Here's
The Heart Wo

MW01267784

"This is a ___ caregiver – and I emphasis CARE. Shannon leads us down the path that we will all take with our parents or will have our children take with us. If you want to share mutual dignity and respect with your children and your parents this is a must read. Love is caring being revealed."
- James Collister, Author of *The Last Relationship Book You'll Need* and founder of Excel In Living Institute.

"In this increasingly more common situation, the story is often one of regret and missed opportunity. Here we see an ordeal accepted as adventure and more than one life transformed. Remarkable."
- Tricia Kelly, *Consciousness Facilitator Trainer*"

I was captivated from the very first page of this book. The opening story of life's synchronicities leading the author on a new path in her life sets the stage beautifully for the insights she shares in living a richer experience through caring. Shannon provides us with tools that give us all the opportunity to live a fuller expression of ourselves."
- Kirk Moore, Author of *Tara's Angels-One Family's Extraordinary Journey of Courage and Healing*, and *Touched by Tara*

"Anyone who is worried (or sure) that their successful life is still missing something should read this book immediately! In every chapter, this poignant, coming of (middle) age story seems to prick at the reader's own complacency. If anyone should read this without chuckling often or losing a few tears, they should check for a pulse!"
- Ruth Ann Hattori, Author of *Innovation Training*, Co-Founder of Innovation Network

"It's through Shannon Ingram's deeply personal recounting of her journey to care that we should all take note that the course of our lives can change drastically in a moment. The ride may be terrifying, heartbreaking, hilarious and peppered with regret and second thoughts, but, ultimately, it will be gratifying as long as you embrace the change with love and compassion. Shannon's transformation will be a warm blanket to the millions of boomers out there facing the same harsh reality—their parents are no longer the indestructible superheroes of their youth. "
- Shelley Gonzales, freelance editor and writer.

"Shannon's book provides proof that leaving an excellent job and moving to another state to care for aging parents can become a blessing and not a sacrifice. Her book is an inspiration: change that includes a positive attitude is life-enhancing. She never preaches . . . she teaches through her own experiences, many of which are delightful."

- Bobbie Probstein, Author of *Return to Center and Healing Now,*
A Personal Guide through Challenging Times.

"A must-read for anyone feeling challenged by the daunting task of elder care. Shannon's heartfelt story offers great insights from lessons learned along the way as she strives to achieve a balance in her both inner and outer worlds."

- Carol Edmonston, Author of *Connections – the Sacred Journey Between Two
Points and Create while You Wait…A Doodle Book for All Ages*

"Sharing her personal journey with humor and honesty, Shannon touched my heart and opened my eyes. Her story is filled with wisdom and compassion—pointing to what matters and the possibility of a truly meaningful life."

– Margaret McIntyre, Management Consultant

For Jenny —
With much
love & LIFE

Shannon

THE HEART WAY

A JOURNEY FROM CORPORATE TO CARE

BY

Shannon Ingram

Orren
Stewart
Press

Costa Mesa, California

. . . .

Dedicated to my parents,
Marianne and Jack Garner and the late John J. Sumner

PUBLISHED BY ORREN STEWART PRESS
Costa Mesa, California

All contents
Copyright © 2005 by Shannon Ingram
All Rights Reserved
No part of this book may be reproduced or transmitted in any
form or by any means, electronic or mechanical, including
photocopying, recording, or by any information storage and
retrieval system, without permission from the author, except
for the inclusion of brief quotations in articles and reviews.

For further information
www.ShannonIngram.com

Cover and book design by Anne White, awhiteink.com,
Huntington Beach, CA

Printed in the United States of America

First Edition

ISBN: 0-9770772-0-9

Library of Congress Control Number: 2005906143

10 9 8 7 6 5 4 3 2 1

INTRODUCTION

This is a book about my journey from the exciting, high-pressure, anxiety-ridden world of corporate America to the quiet, humbling, angst-filled world of caregiving for elderly parents. In January 2003, I left a thriving 25-year career in corporate marketing communications for what I initially thought would be a brief time-out to care for my mom.

Like most executives, I had a plan. I would assess my mom's situation and head a team to manage her care. Then I would find a new corporate position and let the care team handle Mom while I went back to my familiar turf in a window office or on the road with my laptop.

My plan fizzled like the infamous New Coke. I researched caregiving by reading books and articles, surfing the Internet and talking to friends and associates who were caring for elderly parents. I prepared a budget and timetable for plan implementation. In a classic marketing misstep, I failed to consider my emotions and personal response to having an abundance of free time to spend with my mom and stepdad. When I stepped out of the corporate world and into the world of care, I found myself.

In 2003, syndicated columnist and best-selling business author Chuck Martin, chairman and CEO of NFI Research, sent a questionnaire around to members of his global think tank asking if any of us wanted to comment about how to achieve work-life balance. I sent him a response and a couple of months later Chuck used my quote in the online newsletter, Darwin-Information for Executives. The article was titled, *Work-Life Balance: Getting it Right*, and the first line in the article was "The balance between work and personal lives is dramatically out of sync." He related results of a survey of executives and managers in hundreds of US businesses that found less than one percent of people in business believed their lives were extremely balanced in terms of work and personal life. I read the article at least three times, each time feeling better about my current choices and my failed plan to get back on the career track.

Chuck Martin went on to write a wonderful business fable titled *Coffee at Luna's—Three Secrets to Knowledge, Self-Improvement, and Happiness In Your Work and Life*. I went on to write this book about my journey to balance my personal and professional lives.

Part One is the story of putting my career on hold to become a caregiver. *Part Two* is about the "footprints" on my journey—the eight qualities that served me in blazing a trail to care.

Ultimately, I learned that we do not have to abandon our careers in order to achieve balance and demonstrate love for our families and friends. We simply have to care about family, friends, work, and most importantly, about ourselves.

PART ONE

THE HEART WAY

ONE
HEEDING THE CALL

Unfortunately, we often simply tune out the longings we feel, rather than confront and act on them. Perhaps we do not really forget our calls but we fear what they might demand of us in pursuing them.
- Gregg Levoy

Have you ever felt sick of your career or your job and wanted to do something more fulfilling and rewarding in ways other than monetary? Did you — like most of us — put those thoughts out of your mind? Or did you heed your intuitive call and break away from your humdrum or high stress existence to follow your heart?

I left my successful and exciting career in marketing and communications in January, 2003 and moved with my husband, Gary, from Colorado to California to care for my elderly parents. The events of September 11, 2001 spurred me to become more involved with my family, to find a better way of showing my love and appreciation for them. I thought I could do that from Colorado, but after spending a few weekends with my parents over several months, I realized they needed more attention than I could offer long-distance.

My mom, Marianne, suffers from auto bifarct dementia, the result of mini-strokes that have occurred from time to time over the past 10 years. She also has bipolar disorder, which complicated things because she cannot take the drugs that are useful in treating dementia. Mom's doctors said that drugs such as Aricept and Reminyl can sometimes trigger mania in bipolar people, so it's best just to let the dementia take its course.

When I started my frequent trips from Denver to Newport Beach in the spring of 2002, I discovered that Mom had not paid her bills for months. As a result, the phone at her Palm Desert vacation condominium was disconnected and she lost the telephone number that had been hers for over 25 years. The homeowners association for the desert condo was about to foreclose because she had not paid her dues.

My brother, John, his second wife, Linda and their infant daughter lived about 20 miles away from my parents. They had been trying to help with the bills for several months. Linda would drive down to Mom's apartment, go through the bills and write checks for Mom to sign. She would balance the checkbook. And finally, she would stamp the envelopes and leave them for Mom to mail.

Instead of mailing the envelopes, Mom had

been taking them to her bedroom and dumping them into a cardboard box in the back of her crowded closet. I had discovered this box of stamped envelopes on my first spring visit. There were about four months of payments in the box. When I questioned her about it, she said she didn't know how they got there.

My stepdad, Jack, is as sharp as a tack, but his body is home to serious diseases—prostate cancer, macular degeneration, diabetes and congestive heart failure. In 2002, with most of his vision already gone, he was still driving around in his Lincoln Continental.

Jack was relying on Mom to pay the bills, because that's how they had always done things. He had no idea she was no longer competent to do the task. He was also leaving Mom alone in their apartment at the beach for as long as two weeks at a time while he went to stay at his ranch in the mountains. The ranch is about two hours away and it's where my stepsister, Meg, Jack's daughter from his first marriage, lived with her family.

After observing the family dynamics over the course of four weekend visits during the spring and summer of 2002, it was apparent to me that John and Meg had too many distractions to notice what was really going on with our parents, let alone care for them. Each of them had young children, time-consuming jobs and very busy lives.

The difference between my siblings and me was that I had no children. My stepson, Cory, was 27 years old, married and living in Cleveland. My husband was semi-retired. I had a fabulous job as a regional vice president of marketing for a corporate travel management company and I did not want to leave it. But I am the oldest child, a recovering control freak who has always been emotionally attached to my family, no matter how dysfunctional it is.

When I realized the extent of the problems plaguing my parents in California, I decided it was time to care more about them than about my job with all its perks. I was being called to California to care for them, no matter what the consequences were for my prosperous career.

My relationship with my mother has always been good, in spite of its ups and downs. When I was very young, she was my idol – loving, creative, pretty, talented and funny. She was a tall, raven-haired beauty who reminded my friends of Jacqueline Kennedy. She tried unsuccessfully for 11 years to conceive a child and I was the lucky first-born. When people asked me what I wanted to do when I grew up, I would always say, "I just want to live with my mommy."

By the time I graduated from college in 1974, Mom was suffering from serious mood swings that eventually led to a diagnosis of bipolar disorder. I still loved her deeply, but I never knew when she was going to lose her wild Irish temper. She felt threatened by my growing independence, and I wanted to get away from my irksome existence in order to live my own life.

Moving to a different state was good for our relationship because the physical distance brought us together in spirit. Over the years, my mom had remained my best friend through thick and thin, and now she needed me to come home.

On a Monday night in late September 2002, Gary and I went to a sports bar near our home in Parker to watch Monday night football. I had returned from California the previous night. On the flight home, I wondered how I could break the news to him that I wanted to return to California. He is a fourth generation Coloradoan with a deep love for his mountain state and especially the Denver Broncos. Yet he wasn't tied to a job the way I was, and he had always enjoyed our trips to California. Once he even mentioned that it might be a nice place to retire. I just didn't know how serious he was about that.

I had a beautiful view of the Rocky Mountains from the windows in my office in Englewood. On that particular Monday, I caught myself gazing at the mountains during telephone conversations and even while sitting at my computer. I decided I had to summon the courage to talk with my husband that night, since I hadn't been able to do it the night before. If I waited any longer, I might change my mind.

So there we were at our favorite sports bar, Gary puffing on a cigar while nursing his Pepsi and me with a frosty martini and four olives. I took a sip of the martini and began sharing the stressful circumstances of the past weekend with my parents.

He was already immersed in the football game, but seemed to be hearing some of what I said. He would utter an occasional "yep" and shake his head up and down or sideways, his eyes glued to the big screen. I ate two of the olives, heaved a sigh and took hold of his left arm.

"Please look at me," I said, tears welling in my eyes.

"What's the matter?" Gary asked. "What did I do?"

"You didn't do anything. This past weekend, I realized that I have to move back home to the beach to take care of Mom. She deserves a better life than the one she is living right now and I want to help. Maybe I can help Jack, too."

Gary put his cigar into the ashtray, placed a hand on my shoulder and with the other hand, dabbed my tears with a cocktail napkin.

"I'm with ya, Babe," he said. "Say the words and we'll sell the house and move to California. It will be an adventure — another new chapter in our lives, right? I mean, why the hell not do it?"

I took a deep breath and felt a sense of peacefulness that comes from feeling truly committed to a cause. My husband's unconditional support reaffirmed my commitment and resolve. The decision had been made. Our animated conversation focused on things we'd need to do to move forward with this plan. When dinner was finished, we decided not to stay and watch the game. We paid our tab and went home to create a timeline.

TWO
PLANS CHANGE

*Things turn out best for people who make the
best out of the way things turn out.*
- John Wooden

Gary and I had planned to wait until spring
or summer of 2003 to move to Newport Beach.
That would give us time to sell the house, line
up jobs in California and find a place to live, but
the universe had other plans for us.

In October 2002, I decided to share my plan
to move with my boss and one of my executive
peers as part of doing everything in my power to
obtain an inter-company transfer to California. I
thought I had a good chance because the woman
who had my job in the California division lived
in Aspen, Colorado and commuted to California.
My hope was that she would consider swapping
the California territory, or even a part of it, for
the Rocky Mountain Region.

Within a few weeks of these conversations,
it was apparent that no transfer would work out,
for a variety of reasons. The woman in Aspen
did not want to give up the lucrative California
market and her longstanding relationships
with her clients. I asked about the possibility
of telecommuting and working for the Colorado
headquarters office in a business development
capacity. Although everyone I spoke with said
that it would be a shame to lose me, no one
was willing to find me a job. The bottom had
dropped out of the corporate travel market after

9/11, and I had to believe that my inability to secure a transfer was a part of that. To think that I was simply being cast aside was, well, unthinkable.

By the middle of January 2003, too many people knew I was planning to move to California. Even I realized that it wasn't a healthy situation for the company because my employees were depressed about it. I was not surprised to get a call from my boss to come to her office.

She did her best to make the severance easy for me, but I was still crushed. Here I was, sitting in front of a wise and brilliant woman who had taught me a lot about grace under fire. I owed it to her and to myself to take responsibility for my situation. No matter how painful it was to leave, I felt compelled to demonstrate what I had learned from her and bid farewell with the highest and best intentions for all concerned.

The early departure from my job signaled it was time to put the house on the market and get moving a few months earlier than we had planned. Gary, who had been working as a real estate appraiser for the past two years, called his best friend, Pete, in Long Beach, California, to let him know we were moving to his area. Pete astonished Gary by asking him if he would be interested in joining his general contracting business. They had a long conversation about it, and when it was over, Gary had a job waiting for him in Southern California. I had a feeling that the universe was definitely working in our favor.

We flew to Orange County in late January and looked for a house to buy. My parents were ecstatic that we were moving to be closer to them, although they had a hard time believing it was actually happening. When my sister, Meg, realized we were really intent on moving, she called our hotel with good news. Her tenants at a family property on Lido Isle, a beautiful bayside community in Newport Beach, were moving out after nine years.

I had lived in the house on Lido for several years in the late 1980s with my first husband, Bruce Stewart, and had loved every minute because the island is in Newport Harbor and very close to the ocean. Bruce was a yacht captain who had always wanted to retire to the mountains and we moved to Colorado in 1993 so he could realize his dream. Sadly, Bruce died of a heart attack in April 1995, but he had achieved his goal of living on a big piece of property in the mountains. He was laid to rest at Ft. Logan National Cemetery in Denver near the mountains he loved.

After Meg's call to us at the hotel, Gary and I drove to look at the house on Lido. I asked him to be honest about whether he would be comfortable living in a house that Bruce and I had shared. He walked around the entire property, a tiny beach bungalow that was dwarfed by the big renovated homes all around it.

When he was back at the front door where I stood, he said, "I think it's the right thing to do, Shannon. It would be good for us to move in here for awhile and then decide where we want to live permanently. I don't know enough about the area to say where I want to live, and I don't really like any of the places we have seen so far.

It's much more expensive to live in this area than I thought it would be."

We knew our home in Colorado would sell for much less than we would have to pay for a similar home in Southern California. Still, Gary was right. California property was more expensive than I thought it would be. Property values in this part of Orange County seemed to be rising in cost while others were leveling off or even dropping slightly. In the winter of 2003, Southern California real estate was bucking the national trend.

We called Meg and told her we would like to rent the family home on Lido. On the flight back to Denver, we decided our moving date would be February 27, 2003, our fourth wedding anniversary. Once again, we commented that the universe makes no mistakes. We knew we were doing the right thing, with our hearts leading the way.

THREE
THE LONG WAY HOME

You must do the thing you think you cannot do.
- Eleanor Roosevelt

The month of February 2003 was filled with activity: we held a garage sale, donated items to local charities, and took several trips to the city dump with the junk that was beyond donating. We hired a moving company, got the cat and dog ready for relocation with updated shots and vaccines, and attended wonderful parties in our honor.

The hardest part of moving was leaving our dear friends and neighbors. I left more than one going-away party in tears and Gary would suggest, "Think about all of our friends in Orange County," and that stemmed the flow.

I had many friends in Orange County because so few people ever leave the area. Many were former high school pals, and some were people that I had worked with in earlier years. I had introduced all of these friends to Gary before we were married and they had welcomed him into our circle. We felt blessed to have a "safety net" of friendship waiting for us.

The Denver area real estate market was nothing like Orange County that year. We had to reduce the selling price of our home the fourth week it was on the market. By the time our moving date arrived in late February, the house was still not sold. Our realtor and friend, Peggy, assured us she would find a buyer soon, but that it might be closer to springtime when the house finally sold. We appreciated Peggy's honesty and believed the house would sell with or without us in it. The move went off as scheduled.

Gary planned to drive his truck to California with Vanna, our 45-pound blonde shepherd mix, as his "navigator." Our son, Cory, agreed to fly to Denver from Cleveland and drive my car, teaming with his dad on the long trip. Their plan was to leave on February 25th, the same day that I would fly to Orange County with our 12 year-old 21-pound cat, Poudre, who was not a good traveler.

Poudre had never flown before, but I knew any kind of travel would not be easy for him. I had driven him to Colorado ten years earlier and I dreaded taking him on another long road trip. The vet concurred and together we decided that the big fella would travel with me on the plane in one of those soft-side carriers that would fit under the seat in front of me.

Vanna was easy. She loved to go "bye-bye" and Gary made a nice bed for her in the back seat of his truck cab. We planned that Gary would deliver Poudre and me to the airport and then return home to load up the two cars and hit the road with Cory and Vanna so they could arrive in Newport Beach in time for our wedding anniversary, two days later.

The new, post 9/11 security procedures at Denver International Airport proved to be a big challenge for me and Poudre. Although Poudre had taken some "kitty downers," he was still screaming when we left the house, his loud, part-Siamese meow piercing the air in the truck on the way to the airport. "I don't envy you this trip, Shan," Gary said. I assured him that I would get through it, but inside I was feeling very anxious.

At the United counter, I showed the agent Poudre's health certificate and paid for his $80 ticket, which seemed like a lot for a cat. The agent commented that Poudre was bigger than most of the dogs she booked on the planes. She was a bit concerned about whether he could fit under the seat. "He curls up into a little ball when he goes to sleep," I said, trying to convince everyone, including myself that he would settle down soon. She shrugged and handed me our boarding passes. I picked up the heavy kitty carrier and headed for the security screening area in the main terminal.

The security lines were very long, snaking around the terminal. Poudre meowed constantly, which amused some travelers and dismayed others. He was very heavy for me to carry along with my purse. I had checked my small suitcase in order to meet the new carry-on requirements. My only carry-on was a great big cat.

When we passed through the second checkpoint and approached the X-ray machines, I started to put the kitty carrier on the belt. One of the security personnel yelled at another to stop the belt. He came over and grabbed the kitty bag.

"You can't put an animal through the machine," he said.

"OK, then can you just take his carrier with him in it and search it on the other side?" I asked, trying to make it seem simple and logical.

"No, you will have to take the cat out of the bag, put the bag through the X-ray machine and then carry the cat with you to the other side."

"I don't think I can do that," I said, imagining Poudre digging his back claws into me and escaping at high speed into the far corners of the enormous terminal building.

"Well, then you will have to leave your cat behind," he said without emotion.

I could feel the heat in my chest welling up and flushing my neck and cheeks as a lump was starting to form in my throat. I set the carrier down on the metal table next to someone's laptop and opened it, lifting Poudre out. He looked stunned and terrified, even with his eyelids at half-mast due to the drugs. True to form, he dug his claws into my stomach, piercing through my sweater and into my skin. I hardly even winced, keeping a tight grip on him and talking quietly in an effort to calm him and keep him from jumping out of my arms.

"That poor cat," I heard someone say.

"Why would anyone bring a cat on a plane?" said someone else. For a split second, I wondered if I was doing the right thing by taking him with me. Maybe I should call Gary to come and get us right now and drive to California. And then the screener motioned for us to come through the screening device.

We made it through and waited for the carrier to come out on the other side. Poudre was clinging to me like a baby, with his front paws around my neck. "Could you help me get the cat into the carrier?" I asked one of the security personnel. "You will have to wait ma'am because we're very busy." I took another deep breath and said to Poudre, "This part is almost over, Buddy." He seemed to have calmed down a bit but his back claws were still imbedded in my skin.

A shoeless gentleman in a suit came through the screener and said, "I'll help you." He got the carrier and held it open while I disengaged Poudre's claws from my skin and my sweater and placed him inside, zipping the top shut. I thanked the kind stocking-clad man, and collected my own shoes, purse and nerves. At last we were headed for the departure gates.

The rest of the trip was easier. I went to the ladies room to investigate the sore spots on my tummy. Sure enough, there were some perfect, bloody claw marks. Fortunately, I was wearing a dark red sweater. I didn't want to risk infection, so I carried Poudre with me to the terminal newsstand and purchased some antiseptic, then went back and disinfected the sores, which were now stinging noticeably.

I had been booked in an aisle seat. The plane was full, and after I sat down and tried to get Poudre under the seat in front of me, I realized that the space under the middle seat was significantly bigger. I asked the passenger next to me if she would mind switching seats and luckily she agreed. The flight attendant told us this was the first time she had ever heard someone ask to switch to a middle seat.

Poudre was meowing again. I reached into my purse and pulled out a plastic case of foam ear plugs that I had purchased to distribute to my seat-mates, including the people in front of us. Everyone laughed and said they were okay with the loud cat sandwiched between my feet.

As the plane picked up speed during takeoff, Poudre began rapidly turning around in a circle inside his carrier, like a whirling dervish massaging my ankles. I laughed uncontrollably even as I feared that he might be committing suicide on the spot. I tried bending down to touch him through the soft side of the bag, but it was too hard to reach him with the centrifugal force at takeoff. He just kept whirling around, maybe 40 or 50 times, and then suddenly he was still.

When the plane reached its cruising altitude, Poudre was still and quiet, so I opened the bag a bit and reached inside to pet him. The poor cat was panting and his eyes were as big as saucers. I decided it was a good time to simply let his experience be what it was and stop worrying about it. He was alive, quiet and nobody needed earplugs. For the remainder of the flight, I read a magazine, sipped water and tried not to think about the claw marks in my skin.

When we landed at Orange County, I pulled out Poudre's carrier and set him on the aisle seat. Looking inside, I could see that he was dazed, but at least he wasn't frothing at the mouth and his eyes were alert. He kept opening his mouth as if to meow, but nothing came out. Apparently, he had lost his meow.

My brother, John, picked us up at the airport. We stopped by Mom and Jack's apartment to say hello. Jack was at the ranch, so Mom asked if she could go with us to the Lido house. We asked her if she wanted to have dinner with us, and she was delighted to accept.

When we arrived at the house, I let the cat out of the bag. I had thought about confining him to a bathroom, but something told me he would remember his surroundings. Poudre had spent the first year of his life in this home with Bruce and me 10 years earlier. Before Poudre and I had departed Colorado, the vet told me that some animals seem to sense they have been somewhere before, and yet many others do not.

Poudre knew where he was. He was very calm as he sniffed his way from room to room, walking low to the ground and not showing any fear. I put his litter box in the same spot it had been when we had lived here years earlier. And after giving him some food and water, Mom, John and I left for a little family celebration at The Crab Cooker, one of our favorite local restaurants.

Poudre and I spent the night on an air mattress in the master bedroom covered by a sleeping bag that my sister had left for us. Poudre had settled down enough to sleep on the mattress with me and although he still could not meow, his purr was in good working order. We were both exhausted. After talking via cell phone with Gary and Cory spending the night in Grand Junction with Vanna, we drifted to sleep and did not awaken till the sunlight spilled in through the bedroom windows.

I left Poudre at the house and walked over the Lido Isle Bridge to the local Starbucks for coffee and a scone. It was a gorgeous morning and the bay was as still as a big piece of blue glass. Once again I had the feeling that I was in the right place at the right time.

When I had left Newport Beach nine years earlier, I was anxious to get away from what I thought was overcrowded, expensive, shallow Southern California. I despised the changes that had taken place over the previous 20 years – the big buildings, skyrocketing real estate prices and "posers" with their fancy cars. In 1993, I had longed for the charming little beach town that I had grown up in during the 60s. Yet here I was in 2003 appreciating the diversity, the beautiful weather, the fragrance of the salty air, the cars and boats, and the colorful crowds in the OC. I was home.

FOUR
BACK TO THE BEACH

The family is one of nature's masterpieces.
- George Santayana

Gary, Cory and Vanna arrived at the Lido house around 8p.m. on February 26th. That day they had driven all the way from Grand Junction battling snow and ice to contend with as they came through Utah. They chose not to stop in Las Vegas. Gary didn't want me to stay alone another night, especially because the next day was our anniversary. I was thrilled to see them.

After the upheaval at our Colorado home during the previous month with all the packing and down-sizing, Poudre and Vanna, who had never been the closest of friends, seemed genuinely happy to see one another. Poudre head-butted Vanna's right front leg and Vanna sniffed his butt, wagging her tail. Although the Lido house was new to Vanna, I told Gary and Cory that Poudre was letting her know that everything was okay here and we'd be settling down soon. They told me I was nuts and we all chuckled watching the two animals dance around each other during this lovely evening in our patio courtyard.

The following day was our anniversary, the day we had planned to start our new life in California. Around 5:30 a.m., we awakened on the air mattress – sort of. It had lost a lot of its air during the night under the weight of the two of us plus the dog and cat. We had been sleeping on the hard floor for a couple of hours and it wasn't easy to get up. Thankfully we did not have to yell for help to Cory in the guest room to come and get us off the floor.

With luck and good weather, the movers would arrive in two more days. In the meantime, Gary promised that he would inflate the air mattress to the max before we went to bed again.

We spent the day unloading tools, boxes and suitcases that the boys had brought with them in the two cars. We made a couple of trips to Home Depot to get touch-up paint, a wallpaper removal kit to deal with the floral prints on the bathroom walls, and mini-blinds for the kitchen windows. Cory hooked up my computer. The phones were already working and so was the cable TV. I couldn't imagine Gary surviving a day without a TV remote in his hand, so the television had been a big priority.

That evening, the three of us drove over to my parents' apartment and picked them up to go out for dinner to celebrate our anniversary. Jack had returned from the ranch and was thrilled to welcome us home to California. And they looked adorable, Jack decked out in a coat and tie and Mom in her best silk pantsuit and her diamonds. We went to an Italian restaurant in Costa Mesa and were joined by my brother, John, and his older daughter, Lindsey, who was 15.

Lindsey had mixed feelings about our move to California. My niece had been coming to visit me in Colorado every summer from the time she was very young. She loved her escapes to the mountains and wasn't sure that she wanted them to end.

In 1993, the first year that Bruce and I lived in Colorado, Lindsey, age six, flew alone from her home near Palm Springs and spent a week with us. We were living in Conifer, a small town in the mountains about a 45 minute drive from Denver. This was Bruce's dream home — a log cabin with a loft master bedroom, an authentic wood stove in the living room, big windows, and lots of land.

Lindsey loved being a country girl for a change. On the first day of her visit, we went to Sheplers Western Wear and bought her a tiny pair of red cowboy boots, a Levi skirt and a cowboy hat. She wore that outfit the entire week. I took a treasured picture of her sitting on the split-rail fence with our house and pine trees in the background.

Lindsey learned to ride a pony that week, thanks to a neighbor who had horses. I would walk Lindsey and the pony around the dirt roads in our neighborhood and she would wave at anyone who appeared in a window or front yard.

Over the next few years, Lindsey visited for longer periods of time. She and her parents, John and Nancy, flew over to help me move from Conifer to Parker after Bruce's death in the spring of 1995. John and Nancy divorced the following year, when Lindsey was eight.

In the summer of 1998, Lindsey came for the entire month of July. By then, I had met Gary and the three of us had a great time exploring the mountains together. During the days when I was at work, Lindsey spent time with my good friends, Michael and LuAnn, and their baby twins, Ian and Nicole. I drove Lindsey to their home in Denver every morning and then picked her up on my way home. It was a long way out of my way, but I was happy that LuAnn enjoyed having the help and Lindsey loved getting to know the toddlers.

When it was time for Lindsey to go home to California at the end of the month, she had mixed emotions. She was anxious to see her mommy and daddy, but she loved her "second home" in Colorado. She asked if she could come back the next year and I assured her that it would be fine.

The next year Gary and I were married. By the time Lindsey returned in July, 1999, Gary was in the real estate appraisal business. He agreed to "hire" Lindsey to be his assistant and paid her $5 an hour. She accompanied him on his rounds during the day while I worked at my office. It was much easier than driving her to Denver every morning and it gave her the opportunity to get to know her "Uncle G."

When I came home at the end of a workday, invariably the two of them would be sitting out on the backyard deck, discussing politics, boys or music. This was the first time in my life I felt as if I had a family at home, and I treasured every minute of Lindsey's visit.

We continued hosting her every summer, sometimes for a month and sometimes for a week. I thought she would want to stop coming when she became a teenager, with summer school and friends to keep her busy at home. But no, she always came and we always had fun. Lindsey told me that her visits to Colorado had given her something to look forward to when she was sad about the breakup of her family.

In the summer of 1999, we traveled to the Florida Keys on a "family vacation" with Lindsey and her girlfriend, Sydney. The following summer, we took Lindsey and met Cory and his fiancée, Emilie, for "A Taste of Chicago" and a visit to American Girl Place, home of her favorite doll. And the next year we traveled to London and Paris over Spring Break with Lindsey, Cory and Emilie.

Lindsey's reaction to the news of our move to California was subdued. We talked about it during a phone call a couple of days after we had made the decision. She said, "I'm glad that you will be closer to us, but I am sad that I won't be able to come and see you in Colorado. Please forgive me for not being more enthusiastic."

We eased her sadness by telling her that we could all travel to Colorado for vacations. Our friends would still be there and Uncle G was not giving up his Broncos.

At Maggiano's Restaurant that night for our anniversary party, Lindsey raised her glass of soda and proposed a toast, "To Auntie Shannie and Uncle G being close by at last." And then she looked at Cory and added, "And now if we could just get Cory and Emilie to move out here, everything will be perfect." Everyone laughed, but I knew the minute she said it that it was indeed a possibility.

FIVE
FROM BAD TO BETTER

Stop thinking in terms of limitations and start thinking in terms of possibilities.
- Terry Josephson

Emilie arrived in Newport Beach on Saturday, the day after our anniversary, to spend the weekend with us. She was working as a bank teller in Cleveland and took her job very seriously. They needed her income because Cory had been out on disability from his job as a pilot for Continental Express.

The previous 18 months had been very stressful for them. Cory had a couple of close calls as a pilot, including an engine failing at 25 thousand feet and a near-collision on a runway at a major airport. Emilie had been robbed at the bank. Their apartment in Cleveland had burned down, sparing them and their cat, Snickers. They had to live with friends for several months while the apartment was rebuilt.

When they were told it was okay to move back into the renovated unit, it turned out that not quite all the work had been completed. The landlord told them to move in anyway because the contractors would be finished in a few days. So they moved. Cory left on a trip the next day, and Emilie came home from the bank to discover that the contractors had sealed Snickers into one of the walls. She called Cory in a panic. She was so upset that Cory asked his supervisors to take him off the flight schedule for the rest of his trip so that he could go home and get his cat out of the wall. The cat survived.

And then there was 9/11. Cory was on a trip that week and Gary and I knew that one of his legs was to La Guardia in New York City. That awful morning, Gary and I must have hit the redial button on our phone over 200 times trying to reach Cory on his cell phone. At last he answered and after I stopped sobbing, he explained that he was in Lexington, Kentucky. He and his fellow crew and passengers had been on board the plane at the gate ready to depart, but they were told to stay put.

Like every American, Gary and I were in shock for several days. Emilie was alone in Cleveland relying on the support of her friends, while Cory stayed in Lexington until the FAA reopened the airports. His first flights were to Canada to pick up stranded passengers. For the first time in his life, he felt afraid to be in the air.

They had planned to be married in June 2002 at a beautiful place called Sherman Gardens in Newport Beach. They picked Southern California as a wedding location because so many of my family members lived there. But a lot of things were not turning out the way they expected and they had shared their frustrations with Gary and me in January. We told them to follow their hearts and get married whenever and wherever they wanted to, and not to worry about what anyone else thought.

On February 5, 2002, Cory called us to say he and Emilie were in Las Vegas. They had just gotten married, with Emilie's brother and two other close friends in attendance. We were happy they did what they wanted to do. The stress of trying to make the other plans work out was not worth the reward.

About nine months later, just before Gary and I decided to move to California, Cory called to let us know that he had been on a flight to Montreal and had experienced a rapidly racing heartbeat. When he landed, he had to call in sick, fly home to Cleveland, and let his union representative know what was happening. After several days of tests, his doctor presented him with the diagnosis: anxiety attacks. The doctor prescribed medication and Cory had to be placed on disability. He was told he could not return to flying until he was cleared by a doctor. That meant he had to be free from the anxiety attacks and off the medications for several months. But the attacks continued and his spirits seemed to drop with each one.

By the time we moved, he was clearly depressed. He had tried to find part-time jobs in Cleveland, but nobody wanted to hire someone who might be going back to Continental Express at any time. His great career as a pilot that he had planned and studied for since age ten was being taken away by a brain malfunction that was seemingly beyond his control.

Cory would say things to me like, "I don't know how much more bad luck we can we take," and I would respond, "Consider what you're learning from your experiences, and focus on what is working in your life instead of what isn't." He had a beautiful wife and many people around him who loved him. Seeing the bright side of things was very hard for him.

Cory was still suffering from anxiety when Gary invited him to drive my car to California. During their overnight stay in Grand Junction, Gary asked Cory if he would consider moving to California. Gary's idea was for Cory to come and work with him and Pete in general contracting.

In college, Cory had done carpentry work as a summer job and his dad had taught him a lot about construction. Gary told him that he could learn all about the business from his boss, Pete. When and if he was able to return to his job as a pilot for Continental Express, they would accept his decision to return. At the very least a move to California would give Cory the chance to make some extra money and to live close to family.

It was an attractive offer. Without the Continental Express job, it really did not make sense to stay in Cleveland other than to be close to the friends they had made during their two years there.

When Emilie arrived in Newport Beach on the day after our anniversary, Cory talked with her about the possibility of relocating to California. She agreed that it might be a good idea. Lindsey's toast at our anniversary dinner at Maggiano's the night before was already becoming reality.

SIX
A NEW LIFESTYLE

*Life is a daring adventure or nothing. To keep our
faces and behave like free spirits in the presence of fate
is strength undefeatable.*
                                    - Helen Keller

The moving van arrived at our new home on
Monday March 3rd and by the end of our first
full week in California, we were unpacked and
even had some pictures up on the walls. Gary
started working for Pete on Tuesday. Within a
couple of weeks, he was relishing his commute to
Long Beach early every morning. We had heard
about a big snowstorm in Colorado, so Gary
called our former next-door neighbor, Bruce,
and asked how much snow they had outside.
"At least five feet," Bruce said. "I shoveled three
times yesterday afternoon and I feel like I didn't
even make a dent."
    "Sorry to hear that," Gary said, chuckling.
"I'm driving up Pacific Coast Highway right now
past Huntington Beach. The sun has just come
up and is reflecting off the ocean. There are
dozens of surfers making their way out into the
waves. I can see Catalina Island. It's about 62
degrees already and you will be happy to know
that I am wearing shorts and sandals to work."
    "You dog," Bruce yelled into the phone.
"Don't call me again if you're going to tell me
about your perfect weather." They shared a few
more laughs before saying good-bye. Gary hung
up feeling very happy to be in California.

I had been visiting my parents every
day those first two weeks to learn about their
routines and see how I might be able to help
them with some of their challenges. One of the
first things I noticed was that they had trouble
remembering to take medications, and in some
cases they couldn't remember if they had taken
their pills or not. So early one morning, I
went to the pharmacy and purchased a couple
of little plastic pill dispensers that have the
days of the week imprinted on the top of each
compartment.

Mom was taking six pills a day and I loaded
hers into a small green box. Then I tackled
Jack's. He took 14 pills a day so he got the
bigger clear plastic dispenser. He was also better
at remembering to take his meds and at first he
didn't want me to control the process for him.
By Friday, he seemed to like the convenience of
the dispenser.

By the end of those first two weeks together,
I had a list of things to do for my folks. I would
clean out their closets, cupboards and the
refrigerator. Their cleaning lady had quit, so
I decided to find them another one. I would
get both of them started on using disposable
undergarments because they had been having
occasional "accidents" at night. They both
needed haircuts, so I made appointments for
them to go to the salon. And I would get the
finances straightened out and all their bills on a
payment schedule.

The only problem with my list was it would
take a lot of time to accomplish everything that
was on it. And my intention was to get a job

as soon as I had assessed what needed to be done. Before moving, I had read *The Complete Idiot's Guide to Caring for Aging Parents* by Linda Colvin Rhodes, and learned that my best plan would be to assemble a team of doctors, physical therapists, nurses, caregivers and family members to help with their care.

My plan was to hire a caregiver to come in for a few hours a day to cook, do the laundry and be sure that Mom and Jack took their medications. A physical therapist would help with their exercises to maintain strength and balance. They had not agreed to surrender their car keys yet, but I wanted to get them a driver or to investigate the transportation service offered by the senior center in Corona del Mar.

There was so much to do for my folks that I didn't have time to think about getting a new job, so by the end of our third week in California, I began to consider taking more time off from the corporate world to care for my parents. Gary's new job was providing enough money to cover our living expenses. I had my savings in a 401K that could be rolled over into an IRA. We were still making the monthly mortgage payments on our home in Colorado in addition to paying rent for the Lido house, but I knew that our home would surely sell in a month or two when the weather got better.

By the middle of March, several weeks of getting up every morning and dressing in comfy sweats instead of a business suit had spoiled me. Because Mom and Jack were late sleepers, we agreed that I would have the mornings to myself. This was a whole new experience for

me. I enjoyed taking Vanna for a walk along the
bay front and chatting with neighbors. I met
one of my close friends for coffee and a walk on
the ocean front and out onto the Newport Pier.
It dawned on me that most of my girlfriends here
weren't working at full-time jobs. The flexibility
of getting together for coffee or breakfast was
incredibly refreshing for someone who was
used to rushing off to work by 8 o'clock every
weekday.

Most of all, I realized I didn't miss going to
all those tense, mandatory morning meetings
with staff members or clients. Maybe it was
time for me to take a long time-out from the
corporate world if Gary and I could make it work
financially.

SEVEN
EGO TAKES CENTER STAGE

EGO: The fallacy whereby a goose thinks he's a swan. - Anonymous

The two months of relocation madness that I had experienced from mid-January to mid-March 2003 represented the first time in years that I had taken a lengthy break from a "real job." I began working in an office the day after I graduated from high school in the summer of 1969. I worked as an office assistant at a yacht insurance agency while attending the University of California, Irvine, taking four months off to attend the Semester at Sea program during my sophomore year. After graduation from college, I continued working.

I had some fantastic jobs. I was a marine radio operator in the Virgin Islands for a few weeks before landing the position of Executive Director of the Charteryacht League in 1978. Bruce and I were living aboard a 46' sailboat at the time and my little office was on the dock at the marina where our boat was berthed. I handled public relations and communications for a fleet of over 100 privately-owned charter yachts.

We moved to Hawaii in 1979 and I got a job as editor of *This Week Magazines*, the largest-circulation visitor publication in the islands. I didn't know much about editing at that time, but I convinced the publisher I could write and that my perspective as a "mainland haole" — a newcomer to Hawaii — would be good for *This Week*. A few years later, the publisher wrote me a note that I still have, saying: "You were the best editor *This Week* ever had."

I left *This Week* after six years and started my own PR firm. That lasted for about a year. I decided to bring my "little" clients and join a larger firm that had "big" clients like Sheraton Hotels and Aloha Airlines. During the time I worked for the large agency, I did some freelance writing and met many celebrities including Tom Selleck, who was starring in the Honolulu-based TV series, *Magnum, P.I.*

When I moved back to California with Bruce in 1988, I got a job as Marketing Manager for the Disneyland Hotel, which had just been purchased by the Walt Disney Company. I reported to the Disneyland marketing director. Working for Disney was a dream-come-true for me because I was a lifelong fan of Mickey Mouse and my alter ego, Tinker Bell.

Unfortunately, the Disneyland job was stressful and demanding, but when I felt agitated or nervous, I could take a lunch break that was very different than any I took when I worked for other companies. I would remove my badge, hop on the Monorail over to the theme park, get on Space Mountain if the line wasn't too long, and then scream my guts out. It was liberating —the best possible therapy. Afterwards, I could go back to my office and face tight deadlines and grumpy guests with a sincere smile.

Four years into my tenure at Disneyland, the job was not as much fun as it had been in the beginning. The old-timers who had worked for

Walt Disney and committed to carrying on his dream were retiring and a new crop of managers was coming up the ranks. These were people who had no problem working 80 hours a week and getting paid less than half of what they might make at another company. They just wanted to work at Disneyland.

When I was given a choice of seeking a job at Walt Disney Resorts in Florida or taking a layoff, I took the latter. Bruce had already decided that he wanted to move to Colorado, so in January 1993 I left Space Mountain for the Rocky Mountains.

Colorado offered me the first good opportunity to leave the travel and hospitality industries for the technology sector. I figured that a good marketer/manager with broad experience like mine could market anything, so why not go to work in telecommunications or computers? My friends said, "That's where the money is."

In June 1993, I was offered a job as managing director of marketing communications for a large computer distribution company in Denver called Intelligent Electronics (IE). Within six months, I tripled what I had been making at Disneyland. Bruce told me that we should have moved sooner. I laughed when he told me that he couldn't believe that my career was "paying off like a slot machine."

My job at IE was alternately exhilarating and exasperating. I loved the industry, the playful, relaxed environment and the people. But I knew that the business model for distribution was rapidly changing and things would not be the same for long. Nevertheless, I was committed to staying as long as I could.

That commitment deepened after Bruce's sudden death in April, 1995. I came home late one night to find him dead on the basement floor. He had suffered a heart attack and died instantly. It was a tragedy beyond comprehension and I was utterly unprepared to lose him. My IE "family" took good care of me for many weeks. Hundreds of them showed up at Bruce's funeral, including the CEO and president, who had flown in from the corporate offices in Pennsylvania.

Sadly, by 1997, IE's distribution channels had dried up. Rumor had it that our reseller network division would be sold to a company in Southern California called Ingram Micro and our warehouse division would be liquidated. When a headhunter approached me about a vice president job at a local corporate travel management company, I decided it was time to jump.

Corporate travel might sound glamorous, but it is not. It's a business where you get to deal with far too many crabby business travelers who want upgrades, aisle seats and mileage rewards. If that is not enough, you also have to be subservient to vendors like the airlines and car rental agencies who pay little or nothing for you to be their booking agents.

At the time I started in corporate travel in 1997, every airline was trying to figure out how to cut travel agents out of the loop by getting travelers to book trips via the airline web sites. It was a dog-eat-dog industry. Long days stretched into nights of writing proposals, planning events and traveling around the country doing presentations. The only things that made it truly worthwhile were the people I worked with, and the travel perks. The rest of it was pure stress.

But I didn't want to leave. When I arrived in California to oversee care for my parents, I was still trying to figure out how to be re-hired by the company. I was hoping to return to that familiar life of being emotionally drained, working day and night in order to keep the clients happy and the numbers up. I tried to contact my former boss a couple of times, but she never responded. Thankfully, I connected with a few people from the company who seemed happy to hear from me, and that helped my bruised ego, although it did not get me back in the door.

By the second month of caregiving for my parents in California, I began to realize that my ego was not going to let go of my long business career without a battle. No matter how much I enjoyed spending my mornings hanging out with friends and going for long walks, an inner voice was labeling me a "loser" for not having anything in my planner besides my parents' doctor appointments. The only balance sheet I was reading these days was my checkbook. I had forsaken *The Wall Street Journal* for a little beach paper called *The Balboa Beacon*. My time-out from the corporate world still seemed like a good idea, but my ego was crying FOUL.

EIGHT
UNSETTLING CHANGES

Be the change you want to see in the world.
- Mahatma Gandhi

Gary was enjoying his job working for Pete. They had an excellent general contracting business and Gary didn't mind commuting from Newport Beach to Long Beach and Manhattan Beach. He loved it that the word "beach" was in all his work environments, even if they were miles apart. This was his first winter without snow.

Gary traded in his small truck for a larger one so he could carry tools of all sizes and tow a big trailer. Walking into Home Depot every day made him feel like a little kid in a candy store. It was a life radically different from his 20 plus years with the Postal Service in safety and forensics, and his short career appraising real estate in Colorado. He was finally working at something he felt passionate about and he intended to continue working as long as he could.

I was not nearly as happy. I was very aware that no matter how much I enjoyed being with my parents every day, I missed the challenges, perks and pay that went along with a corporate job. Whenever I got an email message from a friend working for my former employer, I felt little pangs of jealousy and sadness about not being a part of their world anymore.

It was great to take care of my folks, and

God knows they needed me. One of the scariest things about their lifestyle prior to my return was their driving. I had no idea how blind Jack had become until I went with him to an appointment with the eye doctor. The doctor described how macular degeneration was gradually taking away all his eyesight. He said that Jack's eyesight had once been like a rich forest and now that forest had been reduced to a tiny bunch of trees in a barren area of deforestation. When those last trees went, Jack would be totally blind. And although we could slow down the progression of the disease, we could never stop it completely. He ended by saying emphatically, "Jack should not drive."

Mom had been driving even though her reflexes were shot, she had cataracts that limited her eyesight, and her dementia made it hard for her to make quick decisions. I discovered some dents and scrapes of brown paint on the driver's side of her white Ford Explorer and asked her what had happened.

"It was just a post," she said, dismissing me. "I've hit it a couple of times, but it really hasn't hurt anything. We can clean the paint off the car."

"What if you had hit a baby stroller or a wheelchair with someone in it? What would you say about that?" I asked.

"Well, it wasn't, so let's not discuss it." She didn't want to go on, but after a few minutes she gave up. She agreed that she probably should not drive anymore and said, "If you would drive me to my appointments and do our grocery shopping, then I will surrender my car keys."

Jack didn't want to stop driving. He wanted to keep traveling from the beach to the ranch in the mountains to stay with my sister, Meg, and her family, and he didn't want to depend on me or Meg to drive him back and forth. It was a scary scenario, but I felt it was my sister's place to talk with him about it, not mine.

Within a month of arriving in Newport, I was driving both of my parents to all their appointments. Occasionally we would go out for lunch or shopping during the day. At least one evening a week, Gary and I would host them for dinner at our house, or we would go to our favorite Mexican restaurant, Mi Casa.

My sister and I decided if Jack would stop driving, we could meet at a Coco's Restaurant halfway between the ranch and the beach to exchange him between the two of us. In that way, he could continue to spend a week or two every month with the Meg and her family. He could still do all the things he loved to do at the ranch, like feeding the horses and sitting on the porch looking out across the meadow.

When Jack was away, Mom came to our home every night for dinner. I would go and pick her up early in the evening and Gary would drive her home after the meal. We had a lot of fun family nights, and Mom commented that her life was better than it had been in several years.

All my friends complimented me on my choice to come home and care for my parents. A lot of them also added that they could never do what I was doing. In my heart, I knew that taking a time-out from the corporate world to take care of my folks was the right thing to do.

But I felt with every passing day I was losing my identity. My career in marketing had been my life, and now it was fading and I was scared to death to lose that part of me. I felt as if my worth as an intelligent human being had dropped off the charts.

While working for the travel management company, I had become active in an industry organization called The Association of Corporate Travel Executives (ACTE). My company was very supportive of ACTE and I had attended all the ACTE national and international conferences over the past five years. I had been asked to serve on the steering committee for the global conference held in Las Vegas in April 2003. When I left my job, my membership in ACTE stayed with me, so I remained on the committee.

In order to complete my commitment to the ACTE conference steering committee, I had agreed to be an independent travel management consultant for my good friend, Grant, a partner in a consulting firm based in Houston. Before leaving Colorado, I told Grant I had no idea how involved I would have to be with my parents and didn't know if I could offer much support to his company. He understood, and remained very supportive of my desire to balance my new role as a caregiver with my career in marketing and travel management.

Late in March, I traveled from Orange County to Washington, DC to attend an ACTE committee meeting. It had been over two months since I had worn a suit, heels and pantyhose to attend a business meeting. My

fellow committee members were high-powered
corporate travel managers who worked for
Fortune 100 companies. Although I had met
most of them before, this time when I entered
the conference room, my ego seemed to be
putting a choke hold on me. It was screaming,
*You are not supposed to be here because you
don't do this work any more.* I felt small and
insignificant and had trouble finding my voice
to greet everyone.

While one of the managers drew event
flow charts on the white board, I found myself
wondering if my parents had taken their
medications or their dog had peed on the kitchen
floor because they forgot to let him out. I had
a vision of my blind stepdad walking through a
puddle of dog pee and then tracking it all over
the apartment as he had done recently.

"Shannon, what do you think about
this abstract for the session on universally
accepted data standards in business travel
management?" asked the committee chair.

"Um, well, I think it's a great session
plan," I said, like an idiot. I had to take a deep
breath and think hard about that abstract,
which was not easy to do when my mind was
focused on a couple of stubborn octogenarians
out in California and whether or not they had
been able to heat their breakfast cereal in the
microwave. These were the same kinds of
thoughts and feelings millions of working moms
have every day. I had evolved into a parent to
my parents.

Thankfully, I was able to contribute a
couple of salient comments. I was relieved to

get on the plane later that day to fly home to Orange County and jump into my sweats and my relatively new routine of free mornings and busy afternoons with the folks.

NINE
WHO AM I NOW?

Things do not change. We change.
- Henry David Thoreau

A month later, I flew to Las Vegas for the ACTE conference. It had been three months since I had seen former co-workers, as well as my clients and industry associates who were attending the event. As much as I had looked forward to this conference, I found myself wanting to go home on the very first day.

My former associates seemed happy to see me, but only one of them asked if I wanted to meet for a cocktail after a scheduled event. My former clients were nice, too, but they were always joined at the hip with the people I had worked with. I knew the strategy – protect your client from predator competitors and consultants. And now I was labeled as one of those predators, wrong as it was. I felt discouraged, rejected and depleted.

Early on the second day, I was registered to attend a breakout session, but at the last minute decided to skip it and stay in my room and watch the morning news programs. I called my mom and asked if she had taken her meds and she said no, but assured me that she would before noon. Jack got on the phone and asked if I had won any money at the slot machines. I told him that I had not had time to gamble because I had been so busy with conference activities.

When I hung up, I decided to ditch the

late morning trade show too, and walk over to another casino to play video poker. Now my inner dialog was all about getting out of the industry and embracing the business of being a caregiver. Sitting on a stool in front of a slot machine, my fingers pushed the buttons to deal new "cards" while my ego pushed hard against my desire to be a caregiver. What a big loser I was. No wonder I couldn't win at the slots.

My $20 gambling allotment shrank quickly, so I walked back to my hotel, consumed with self-pity and sadness. I was no longer important to this group now that I was not working for any of the big industry players. I decided to skip the afternoon breakout session. Instead, I went up to my room and watched *Oprah*. Somehow I felt that Oprah would understand what I was going through, and that made me feel better.

That night, after my "Oprah-therapy" and a hot bath, I rallied my travel management executive persona and accompanied some former associates from the East Coast to dinner with their clients. We went to one of the fabulous gourmet restaurants at The Bellagio. I was so thankful they had called that afternoon to see if I wanted to join them. After dinner, we stayed in the casino and played the slots and drank martinis. It was great fun and I won $50. I thought to myself, *Well, maybe I've been too hasty thinking I want to get out of this business.*

Grant had arrived late to the conference. On the afternoon of the second day, he found me on the trade show floor. "Have you had any success drumming up business with your former client?" he asked.

"No, but I can set up a meeting with her for you. I know she will meet with us." Again, my inner voice told me that I had no business in this role right now — my work was at home with my parents.

Right before the meeting with Grant and the client, my cell phone rang. It was my mother.

"Did you remember to call and cancel the dog's bath this week? If you didn't, then we are going to get a no-show charge because we had no way of getting him there this morning," she said.

"No, Mom, I did not call them. Why didn't you call them?" I asked.

"I can't find my phone book," she said.

"Did you look in the little drawers next to the phone?" I asked.

"No, but that doesn't make any difference now. We are going to be charged the $20. And Pam called from the desert to say there's a problem with the refrigerator and one of the renters is complaining. What am I supposed to do?"

"Call Meg and ask her to handle the refrigerator in the desert. That's about the best advice I can give you right now."

"Please don't raise your voice, Shannon. I'm sorry to bother you."

"It's okay, Mom," I lied. I wanted to scream at her that I was very busy and not in a place where I could talk about the dog's bath and the faulty fridge. Just then, Grant tapped on my elbow and whispered that the client was already seated nearby. He took off in that direction.

"Shannon, I cannot believe that you're

yelling at me," Mom said. "We are stranded here in the apartment because you're in Las Vegas. Your brother hasn't come to see us at all and Gary only dropped by once. We need some things from the market. What are we supposed to do?" Grant was seated now, smiling and gesturing at me to come over to the table.

"Mom, I really cannot talk right now. I'm in a meeting. I'll call Aunt Carla and see if she can come up and go shopping for you. Remember, you're supposed to call them if you need anything."

"I don't want to bother them," she said.

"OK, let me see if I understand, Mom. You don't want to bother the people who are 15 miles away, but you do want to bother me in Las Vegas, right?"

"Don't get sarcastic with me, Shannon."

I took another deep breath and looked in the direction of Grant and the client. There was no sense arguing with my mom now. "I'll call Aunt Carla for you and she will help you get your groceries. OK? Are you ok now?"

"Yes, but I wish you wouldn't be so impatient with me."

"I'm sorry to be upset. I love you. See you in a few days."

I snapped my cell phone shut and heaved a big sigh. I had to sympathize with Mom. She couldn't possibly see things from my perspective. She could only see her side, which was about the dog and the groceries and the inconvenience of not being able to drive. I resolved to be more empathetic.

I turned around to head to where Grant

and the client were sitting. I felt someone touch
my arm. It was a former associate.

"Hi, how are you? I just overheard your
conversation and it sounds as if you have your
hands full these days. Was that your mother?"

I wanted to say, *None of your business*, but
instead I just said, "Yes it was."

"Well I envy you getting out of the corporate
world, Shannon. Does it feel funny to be here
now that you're at home all the time?" *How
annoying*, I thought. But I said, "It feels just
fine — probably like you with your kids calling
you at work all the time, right? That's how my
parents are for me now, like my children. And
I always answer their calls the way you answer
your children's calls."

"Oh I hadn't thought of it that way, but
you're probably right." She smiled.

"Take care," I said. "I have to run because
I'm late for a meeting with Grant."

For the first few minutes of the client
meeting, I wasn't focused on the conversation at
all. I thought about my former associate's cloying
comments and my nasty comeback about her
talking on the phone to her children. *How dare
she question my reason for being here? And yet
all she was doing was mirroring my own doubt.
I did not want to be here. I did not want to be
in travel management any more, and I no longer
had much in common with any of these people.*
That positive, motivational "Oprah feeling" had
worn off.

At the big celebration dinner in the grand
ballroom on the last night of the conference,
I sat at a head table with the other steering

committee members. As we were acknowledged by the emcee, our names appeared on the big screen and we stood for a round of applause. While standing, I thought it would be more appropriate for me to be receiving applause for convincing my mother to give up driving. That had been a lot more challenging than anything connected with this conference.

Because I never had any children, I had nurtured my career as if it were a child. I threw myself into the business of marketing and communications and took great pride in working my way up the corporate ladder. The problem-solving and office politics I encountered were my experience of parenting—myself and my associates. When my girlfriends who did not have business careers spoke of envying my corporate success, I told them I envied their role as full-time parents. There at the ACTE banquet, I realized that my priorities had changed and that my business career was on hold so that I could nurture my parents.

During the four-course meal, some of the committee members were talking about running for the ACTE Board and tackling big industry issues like airline stability and broader strategic roles for executives responsible for travel management. I thought about the big issue of getting my parents to switch from the kind of undergarments they'd been wearing for most of their lives and begin wearing disposable underwear. Perhaps I could form a Board to advise me about that? Then again, maybe not.

After the banquet, I decided to pass on going out for drinks with committee members and business friends. It seemed inappropriate and unappealing. These people were not interested in me anymore, and I was not very enthusiastic about them, either. I liked them, but business was the foundation of our relationships, and it was past tense. I just wanted to go home. My heart was no longer in the corporate world.

In my room, while packing for my morning flight, I started to cry. No matter how noble it was for me to take care of my parents, it was sad to lose the corporate part of my life. Suddenly I felt bitter and guilty for sitting there crying into my carry-on. At the moment the guilty feeling came over me, my tears stopped.

Surely there is something good about my situation, I thought. *After all, I am much more than the sum of my career in business and caregiving for my parents. I am still the creative, energetic, positive person I was before I left the corporate world. The experience of being a full-time caregiver to my parents is teaching me an amazing lesson about balancing work and making a living with whatever it is that I truly care about in life. I care about my family and friends. I care about education. I care about the environment. I care about making a positive difference in the lives of people I meet. Perhaps the gift in this trip to Las Vegas is for me to embrace the future creative possibilities that I can see through this new, more balanced perspective.*

TEN
BREAKDOWN

One must still have chaos in oneself to be able to give birth to a dancing star.
- Friedrich Nietzsche

The inner drama about losing my identity did not end with my positive thoughts that last night in Las Vegas. It continued to see-saw and percolate, finally reaching a crescendo one day in mid-June. For about a week, I had been journaling about my concerns that I was no longer interested in a high power corporate job, but I didn't have an alternative position in mind. I couldn't decide if I wanted to find a lower-paying desk job without a lot of stress and responsibility so that I could continue to be a part-time caregiver, or try to work from home as a writer, editor or marketing consultant.

My ego had been bruised by the recent conference in Las Vegas. About a week after I got home, I called Grant to say that I couldn't continue to be a travel management consultant. True to his compassionate nature, he said, "That's not a problem. I'm happy to have you come back into the fold if you change your mind."

I loved the weekday mornings at home with my dog and cat, working on the computer in my little office at the back of the house. After an early walk around the island, I returned home each day to sit at my desk for a couple

hours, sipping coffee and catching up on email
or talking on the phone with my girlfriends.

For most of my life, weekday mornings
at home had been rush hours. I don't enjoy
getting up early, so I always stayed in bed as
long as I could. Then I would dash through my
routine of showering, drying my hair, dressing
and grabbing a cup of coffee and a granola bar
for the drive to work. I always did my makeup in
the car stopped at traffic lights, finishing before
I drove into the parking lot.

Having the morning hours to do anything I
wanted to do was a luxury I was learning to savor.
The morning show hosts became my friends. I
kept the TV on in the background while I did
laundry, cleaned the kitchen and made plans
for dinner. Sometimes I caught myself talking
to Katie Couric about something as silly as how
she was blushing while interviewing Harrison
Ford or to Diane Sawyer about a great outfit she
was wearing. It didn't matter to me that they
couldn't hear my comments.

I recall thinking that I was becoming some
sort of stereotypical middle-aged housewife who
talked to the television because no one else was
around. And I liked it that way.

What I did not like was the feeling that
my life was one-dimensional. I missed having
projects to keep me busy – projects besides
taking my parents' little toy poodle to the vet
or cleaning out Mom's bedroom closet or fixing
Gary's lunch every morning.

Shelley, my friend in Colorado, suggested
that I get more serious about writing. That
appealed to me because writing had always been

one of my passions. She said, "You can do it from your home office." She had been a reporter for many years and was very supportive in telling me to pitch an idea to a newspaper editor. I thought it would be fun to write a column called *"Back to the Beach"* about my experience of returning to my hometown after years of being in other states.

With Shelley's help, I pitched the column idea to the editor of a local newspaper. I spent a couple of days writing sample columns and had Gary, Shelley and some of my friends read them. I was encouraged when all of them laughed at my new material. I put together a nice package with hard copies and a CD and delivered it to the newspaper offices in Costa Mesa, a couple of miles from my home.

When I didn't hear from the editor after a few days, I called him and left a message that I was following up. Then I called again. And again. And again. About a week after my first call, I actually reached him in person. He said he had seen the package but had not had time to read my columns because he was busy editing several small coastal city newspapers that were part of the larger newspaper chain. He promised to read them and get back to me. Of course, he never did.

I also tried to reconnect with some of my former co-workers at Disneyland. There were a couple of low-level management jobs posted on the Disney web site that I applied for because I thought it would be fun to work at the Magic Kingdom again. I didn't want to get into higher level management with all of its responsibilities and long work weeks because I still needed time to spend with Mom and Jack.

One of the men I had contacted at Disneyland sent me a two-line email saying, "I am not real involved with this and as you noted we have gone through a lot of changes...Best of luck and I will pass your resume on." In other words, do not contact me again. Another sent a one-liner: "Really busy. Will call you soon." I was devastated by the brush-offs, but I kept telling myself this was a gift from God because deep down, I did not want to go back to the corporate world.

Weeks passed with no job offers. It had been 30 years since I had asked anyone for money and I wasn't about to start now. So instead of asking Gary for money to buy things like clothes and household goods, I decided to use my credit cards.

In 1986 I had gotten into trouble with credit cards and turned to Consumer Credit Counseling to help me clean up my debts. The good news was that I had avoided bankruptcy, and I felt good about that. So this time I promised myself that I would not to spend too much with plastic; but I was not prepared to have Gary tell me that I couldn't afford to buy a new pair of jeans.

I was sick of not having my own income to play with – to put away and save for a vacation, or to spend on something special like a massage or a facial. The cost of living in California was indeed higher than it had been in Colorado. And even though we didn't have to pay the high cost of heating in the winter months, gasoline and groceries were much more expensive than we thought they would be.

The house in Colorado was still on the market and Gary and I were concerned about our decreasing savings. We had already forsaken many of the fun things we had enjoyed in Colorado – dining out at nice restaurants, weekend stays at quaint little hotels or B&B's in colorful towns, and impulse purchases of things like fishing poles, gourmet cookware and cool shoes.

Cory and Emilie had sold their home in Cleveland and were already packing for their move to California in July. They visited us early in June and together we had found a cute little rental home in the Belmont Shore area of Long Beach. Gary and I agreed to help them with some of the financial obligations of the move, like their first and last month's rent.

When I shared my fears with Gary about losing my identity along with my marketing career, and about not having enough money to get by unless we sold the house right away, he said what he always says, "Release it to the universe." Good advice, but easier to say than to do, especially when your inner voice is nagging about lack of everything from money to spiritual growth.

Gary added, "You have much to be grateful for: a beautiful place to live, a family that is coming together again, and many, many good friends." Instead of embracing Gary's comments, I burst into uncontrollable sobs and started yelling at him.

"You can't possibly understand how I feel because everything is going so well for you," I wailed. "I have never given birth to any children. I have not raised a family the way you did. My identity is all wrapped up in my career, and right now I feel completely lost. I have no idea where I'm going and if I did, I wouldn't know how to get there."

He was silent.

My days had changed from hours packed with business conflict resolution, executive committee meetings, brainstorming sessions and client entertainment. Now I spent the hours doing the dirty work of cleaning two houses, scrubbing floors and toilets, walking my parents' untrained and equally ungrateful dog, and driving old people to doctor's appointments. It was not all bad by any means. I was having a lot of fun with my parents, going out to lunch and shopping and sharing stories. I deeply loved them and wanted to continue caring for them; but I missed the old me — the one who wore the elegant suits, handled customer service issues, wrote proposals and coached a great staff of professionals.

My imagination conjured up images of the story of *The Little Princess*. It was about a wealthy little girl who was suddenly forced from a life of luxury at an elite boarding school into living in a dirty attic. She went from being waited on hand and foot to a life of scrubbing floors and toilets because the headmistress learned that the girl's wealthy father had died and left her penniless. But I couldn't imagine a happy ending like the one in the book. I was just stuck in the attic of my mind and my ego. And I was having a major meltdown of profound self-pity and remorse.

When my sobs subsided, Gary was still sitting next to me on the sofa. I was surprised that he wasn't talking. He sat there silently and did not touch me or offer any consolation.

Finally, he said, "Shannon, you are the one who is making the choices here. Nobody is telling you what to think or how to feel about what is going on around you. You wanted to quit your job and move here to take care of your mom. I chose to come with you. But how you feel about your life today is what you're making of it. It has nothing to do with your mom and dad or me. If you're so unhappy, why don't you do something about it? Call your therapist in Denver or find a new church. Maybe you need to seek support from someone besides me. What makes you think that you can care for your folks if you can't care for yourself?" He stood up, squeezed my shoulder and left the room.

As much as I hated hearing that my bad mood was my choice and that I needed to be responsible for my own attitude, I knew Gary was right. Years ago, I heard Wally "Famous" Amos, creator of the Famous Amos brand of chocolate chip cookies, speak at a luncheon in Honolulu. He said something that had stuck with me, "Your attitude determines your altitude." My attitude was in the tank, and it was no wonder that I felt so low.

I pondered Gary's comment about finding a new church. We had enjoyed a rich spiritual life in Colorado. Replicating that in California was not at the top of my agenda when we moved. Perhaps now I needed to make it more important.

I had left my beloved therapist, Marjorie, in Denver, but there was no reason I couldn't talk with her on the phone. Or perhaps I could find a new therapist in Orange County.

My big black planner book was sitting in front of me on the coffee table. I picked it up, opened to the next day's list and made some notes to myself about finding a church, calling Marjorie for counseling and finding a local therapist, tools that would surely support me in navigating the strong current of my identity crisis.

ELEVEN
LIBERATION

Change the way you look at things and the things you look at change.
            - Dr. Wayne Dyer

My big meltdown turned out to be a healthy one. Not only did it facilitate conversations with Marjorie, but it initiated a series of conversations with myself about what was really going on.

Early on weekday mornings, after Gary left for work, I would sit down at the dining room table with my coffee. Instead of reading the newspaper or watching the morning news, I talked to myself and my "angel team" — my grandmother, my father and my first husband. I asked them to help me find solutions to my problems.

I heard Daddy's voice reminding me he had left the corporate world when he was in his forties in order to pursue a musical career. He played guitar, banjo and violin – or "fiddle" as he liked to call it. For many years he supplemented his music gigs with work as a security guard, a property manager and a real estate salesman, whatever he could do to keep food on the table and music in his life.

My maternal grandmother, Alta, whom I called Gammie, had been abandoned by her first husband, Ray. My mother's father left Gammie with three little children to bring up alone. She was consumed with despair for awhile. Then one afternoon while repairing a torn hemline in one of her dresses, she realized she had a talent she could possibly turn into a livelihood. Her gift was designing and sewing beautiful clothing and she also enjoyed creating magical parties. She became the first wedding counselor in Glendale, California. She made all the dresses for her clients' bridal parties, baked the wedding cakes and decorated the reception halls.

Gammie's business supported her children until she met and married her second husband, Mac. He was a successful realtor and widower with three children. Gammie closed her business after she married Mac, but she created beautiful weddings for her three children and three stepchildren, and sewed wonderful clothes for everyone in the family until she could no longer use a needle and thread.

The message I heard from my grandmother was: "Ultimately the only person you control is yourself. You can't find the answers you need without spending time doing the homework necessary to find them. You have to trust yourself."

At first Bruce's voice was so faint, I wondered if he had abandoned me. Then one morning I was in the guest bathroom cleaning the sink and noticed in the mirror a framed print of two killer whales swimming upstream against the current. It was hanging askew on the wall behind me. As I turned around, I suddenly felt as if Bruce was telling me to look into the print. In my mind, I heard him say the whale in the lead represented me, and he was the one who was jumping out of the water a few feet behind me. His message was, "Stop worrying. Keep looking ahead. I've got your back."

As I straightened the frame, I shivered and felt goose bumps forming on my arms. Bruce was telling me to hang that print where I could see it every day. He wanted me to know it was okay to keep moving forward and follow my heart upstream, even if I felt all alone.

For the first time in months, I believed that everything was going to work out fine. In addition to Gary, Cory, Emilie, Lindsey and my close friends, I was blessed with a team of angels rooting for me and helping me to see with my heart as well as with my eyes. In that moment, I completely understood the important connection of body, mind and spirit.

The emotional meltdown of losing my identity left me open to these messages of hope. Ironically, I needed to let go of my practical, analytical self and get a little crazy in order to discover an easier, more peaceful way to adjust to my new way of life without an office or a "real job."

I resolved to take action and chart a path to accepting myself in my new role as a caregiver. Marjorie helped me to see that I was in the grief cycle again. This time it was not about the passing of someone I loved, but the transition out of my life in Denver. I needed to grieve over the loss of my job, my friends, my church, my home and all that I loved about Colorado.

Everything had happened so fast when we decided to move I didn't have time to be sad. It was one, big, prolonged shock period with some excitement about my new adventure thrown in. But now, in June, I finally woke up to the harsh reality I had considered during my stay in Las Vegas two months earlier. My lofty career in business was on hold indefinitely for caregiving, and that had made me angry and depressed.

I could also see my inability to let go of my life in Denver was somehow connected to our house in Denver not selling. At some unconscious level, I was hanging onto the house for dear life. Negative energy was fueling my personal cycle of gloom because it contributed to my financial worries.

As a firm believer of what Dr. Wayne Dyer calls "The Power of Intention," I knew I could let go of all things Colorado if I reframed my new caregiver life as simply another chapter in my career, and not the end of it. It was time for me to shift my perspective to one of possibility and creativity to allow something new and better to unfold.

This new perspective was wildly liberating. By the middle of June, several good things had happened. Our home in Colorado sold. After watching a tragic news report about an elderly man who accidentally ran down dozens of people in Santa Monica, killing 10 of them, Jack voluntarily surrendered his car keys and said he was finished driving. Mom and I decided I could receive a "gift" in exchange for caring for her and Jack. I decided to pursue freelance writing as a way to stay connected to people and information I enjoyed outside the caregiving realm.

I dropped out of ACTE and joined the National Family Caregivers Association. It seemed appropriate to belong to an industry organization within my new career field.

Early in July, I called the Huntington Beach Church of Religious Science (HBCRS) to inquire about its services. I had been a member of HBCRS in 1992 before moving to Colorado. While I was a member, the minister, Dr. Peggy Bassett, had been a powerful influence in my life. Every Sunday, I was inspired to take on almost any challenge that came my way. I took classes from the assistant minister, Dr. Roger Teel, who always spoke fondly of the Mile Hi Church in Denver he had come from before moving to Southern California.

When I moved from California to Denver in 1993, I phoned the Mile Hi Church and told them I had recently relocated from Huntington Beach. The receptionist asked if I knew Dr. Roger. I said yes and she exclaimed, "He's coming back here next month to take over as senior minister." That did it. I started going to Mile Hi the following Sunday and was a member for almost 10 years.

While I was living in Denver, Dr. Peggy Bassett passed away, or "crossed over" as I prefer to think of death, after a courageous battle with ALS (Amyotrophic Lateral Sclerosis, a.k.a. Lou Gehrig's disease). So when I called the HBCRS this time in June 2003, I was simply trying to find out if I wanted to go back. A receptionist told me they were between ministers. She said the church had become smaller in the last 10 years. I thanked her, hung up the phone and decided to listen to my intuition telling me to keep searching for my new spiritual home.

Mom asked me to take her to a church in Newport and we went several times. The music was beautiful, the messages inspiring and the people were very nice; but I did not feel a connection compelling me to return.

It was the middle of summer, so I decided for the time being, my spiritual base would be the little beach at the end of our street on Lido Isle. I went there with the intention of being closer to God. I sat on the sand and meditated on early mornings, especially on Sundays.

TWELVE
MY BROTHER, MYSELF

We're born alone, we live alone, we die alone.
Only through our love and friendship can we create
the illusion for the moment that we're not alone.
- Orson Welles

My brother, John, and I have been close friends since he was born in 1954, two and a half years after me. We shared a bedroom for the first two years of his life and I remember the silly things I would do to make him smile and giggle behind the bars of his crib. Once I brought him a full box of cornflakes which he proceeded to dump into his bed. I climbed into the crib with him to jump up and down on the cornflakes. We laughed hysterically as the flaky dust spilled out onto the floor, making a horrible mess for my mom to clean up.

When he was a toddler, I tried to anticipate everything he wanted. He would point at something and I would get it for him, or I would tell anyone who would listen what he wanted. All he had to do was say, "ah, ah, ah" and point, and I would talk for him. I was so good at it that Johnny wasn't even trying to talk, so at the urging of our pediatrician, Mom sent me to stay with my grandmother for two weeks.

During that time, Mom and our Polish housekeeper, "Baba," worked with John to get him to talk. When I came back from Gammie's house, John had a good start on his English vocabulary, but with a Polish accent thanks to

Baba. Instead of "ah-ah-ah", he would say, "I
von dat googie, peas," and Mom, Dad and Baba
would clap because they knew he was saying, "I
want that cookie, please." All I could say was,
"He sure talks funny."

We shared many adventures, from playing
cowboys on the trail in our backyard to racing
bicycles down the hill in front of our house to
sitting up till late at night under the grand piano
listening to our daddy's band play Dixieland
music. I went to his Little League baseball games
and he sat through my piano recitals. Once,
when I was about 12 and Johnny was 9, our
parents had to attend a funeral, so they decided
that we could go alone to Disneyland for the day.
It was great fun to run around the park and do
anything we wanted. We got into some mischief
on the Skyway buckets that ran on a high wire
cable between Fantasyland and Tomorrowland.
We had bought a huge dill pickle out of a barrel
at a store on Main Street and decided to drop it
onto the pavement from the Skyway. We were
careful not to hit anyone, but we wanted to see
the pickle go splat. All it did was bounce and land
near someone's foot. We hid inside the bucket
laughing and congratulating ourselves. Nobody
caught us and we felt very powerful, whispering
and giggling about our secret bombing run all
the way home that night.

John was a star basketball player. He was
a natural because he was always the tallest
kid in his class. As a senior, I was so proud of
him when he arrived as a freshman in our high
school. By that time, he was very confident,
popular and outgoing. I was still shy, insecure

and nerdy. I asked him to participate in a student/teacher dance contest fundraiser for the school yearbook committee that I was on, and to my delight, he agreed and encouraged some of his friends to join in too. John and his teacher partner won a top prize and my fellow committee members were very impressed.

We shared the difficult times, too. Our parents divorced when we were barely teenagers. It was extremely hard on John because he felt he had to take care of me and Mom. Our father's alcoholism was a battle we could not win. We navigated Mom's mood swings together and supported one another in moving away when we were old enough. John flew to Colorado to be with me after Bruce's death and I helped him get through his painful divorce. Our close bond was always a bridge over troubled waters.

When Mom married Jack and brought Meg into our lives, she became the "little sister" I had always wanted. Even though John, Meg and I were young adults, it was not easy for us to blend families at first. The closeness between Mom, John and me and Meg's background as an only child slowed down the process, but ultimately, the bonds of trust and love grew during holiday family celebrations and traveling to places like Hawaii, Aspen and Lake Tahoe together.

John, Meg and I were in each other's weddings both times (each of us has been married twice), and for John's second marriage to Linda in 1998, he asked me to be his "Best Man." Moving to California gave me the incredible pleasure of getting back together with my wonderful brother and our extended family, and I looked forward to many good times together in the future.

During the six months after my return to California to care for our parents, I realized that John's life was very different than mine. He had a toddler, a teenager and a time-consuming job. No matter how much he would have liked to have been involved with caring for Mom and Jack, he just couldn't do it.

I wasn't angry or resentful because I could empathize with him. I had lived far away from my parents for 20 years and he had always been right there in their backyard. He had done what he could the past couple of years, and for now, in the interest of his own sanity, he needed to step back and let someone else take over. That someone was me.

THIRTEEN
A WINNER VOICE

If you don't like something, change it. If you can't
change it, change your attitude. Don't complain.
- Maya Angelou

Cory and Emilie drove out from Cleveland at the end of July 2003. We helped them move into a quaint little two-bedroom house and get settled with their dog and cat.

Within 24 hours, they were madly in love with their new neighborhood. They called us to talk about all the cool things to do in Belmont Shore. They could walk the dog down to the beach, just a few blocks away, and the ocean breeze made sitting on their front porch a great way to spend an afternoon. They liked their new neighbors, David and Jill. They had no complaints. I told Gary this new chapter in their lives might spell the end of Cory's anxiety attacks.

I was able to join Lindsey for all kinds of fun activities during her week-long stay in July because for the first time in all the years she had been coming to visit, I didn't have a set work schedule. We included Mom and Jack in some of our excursions so Lindsey could get to know them better. At the age of 15, she had never spent as much as a weekend with my folks. The hours we whiled away at their apartment that week were filled with interesting conversation, questions and lots of laughter.

Mom shared stories with Lindsey about

her youthful days attending the University of California at Santa Barbara, living in the dormitory and meeting my father, who was a telephone lineman at the time. Lindsey asked Mom what had attracted her to "Papa John" and Mom thought for a minute. "I guess it was mostly just because he was tall." I started to laugh because several years ago, in grief therapy after Bruce died, Marjorie, my therapist, had asked me to share with her what my parents had in common. For some reason, the only thing I could come up with was, "They were both tall."

I said to Lindsey, "Well, being tall held their marriage together for over 20 years and produced two kids, so I guess that was a good thing."

Mom added, "Your dad was a wonderful, intelligent and creative man. We had such fun together. We both loved the music that he made. But we grew apart as so many couples do. And then I found 'Papa Jack.' He is not quite as tall as I am, but we have been married for 30 years."

We all laughed, including Jack, who said wearing cowboy boots always added a couple of inches to his height. But these days he traded his comfy, flat boat shoes for being a wee bit shorter than Mom.

Late one afternoon, Lindsey and I decided to take beach chairs down to the little stretch of shore at the end of our street. Gary was not home from work yet, but we knew he would join us as soon as he noticed the beach chairs were gone. We took off our shoes, parked chairs in the warm sand and popped the tops on our diet sodas.

Sitting at the beach every evening with Gary had become a ritual. The activity on the bay never ceased to entertain us, from the life jacketed students taking sailing lessons in dozens of look-alike white boats to the enormous wedding and party boats to the elegant old sailing yachts to the bearded guys in kayaks to the jumping fish and the occasional seal. It was one big show every day, right in our own backyard.

On this particular day in July, Lindsey wanted to talk about college. She knew my mother, "Gigi," had started a tuition fund for her a couple of years earlier. But she was worried that she wouldn't be able to afford a four-year college. "I know that Uncle G would say, 'you can do anything you want to do,' but I still have this little voice inside that says 'I can't,' " she said.

"I know that little voice," I said. "You can make it your friend or your foe. It becomes your enemy when you let it bring you down and make you suffer. It's your friend when you can have a conversation with it and say, 'thank you for sharing and I will just keep on moving toward my goal.' After all, it's just your own inner voice. Why not put a "w" in front of it and make it your "winner voice?" Even if it's throwing red caution flags at all of your aspirations, you can take a look at those flags and decide if they are valid, then take more action if necessary."

Lindsey smiled. She liked the "winner voice" idea and so did I. The idea had just popped into my head there on the beach, like a divine inspiration. It was easy to remember. I have always liked the saying, "we teach what we most need to learn," and it occurred to me I needed to heed my own "winner voice" too. Until recently, I had been prone to worry and fear, which was not my style. My style was better suited to reinventing myself when the opportunity arose.

FOURTEEN
MOVING AGAIN

Everything you can imagine is real.
- Pablo Picasso

One of the fears I wanted to tackle with my "winner voice" in the summer of 2003 was about our living quarters. Now that we had sold the house in Colorado, and we were certain that we wanted to live in Orange County near my parents, we knew that it was time to buy a home of our own. We loved the little beach house on Lido Isle in Newport Beach; but it belonged to Meg and her family.

I gingerly broached the subject of asking Meg to consider selling the house to us one day when my stepdad and I were out running errands together. He said she would not go for it. Although I had lived in the house for a total of six years off and on, and Meg had never lived there, Jack said he knew she did not want to sell it to me or to anyone. It was nothing personal.

Meg, Ted and their eight year-old daughter, Hannah, loved the house too. Meg wanted to hang onto it in case she and her family decided to move from the mountains to the beach during Hannah's high school years. So rather than try to change her mind, Gary and I decided to start looking for another house in a more affordable neighborhood than Newport Beach, but still close to my parents' apartment.

The Orange County real estate market was red hot in 2003. We could not believe the prices of little "cracker box" houses in Costa Mesa and Huntington Beach. Nothing met our needs priced under $700,000, which was more than double what we had received for our home in Colorado that summer. We had serious sticker shock, but in the spirit of intention and knowing we were meant to be in California, we knew that we would find a perfect home if we were willing to be patient and creative.

When I told Mom we weren't going to stay in the Lido house and had begun looking at other more affordable neighborhoods in Orange County, she grew very nervous, to the point of gasping, "I don't want you to be too far from us. I like having you just five minutes away."

"I like it too, Mom, but we have to be realistic and we don't want to keep renting, so we have to look at areas where the houses cost less."

"Please don't move to Fullerton," she said, referring to my brother's hometown. "I'll never see you again."

We both chuckled and I reassured her there was no way I was going any farther than a 20-minute drive. After all, I moved back to California to care for her, and it would be hard to respond quickly if I were more than 15 miles away.

"I want you to live in Newport Beach," she said.

"That's very nice, but it's not going to happen. The homes here start at about $1.2 million and we cannot possibly go there." I said.

"Well, then how about Goat Hill?" she said, using the nickname we had always used to refer to Costa Mesa. "It may not be Newport, but it is nearby and less expensive."

"Yes, but Costa Mesa is still way out of our price range. It has become a very cool neighborhood and it's too pricey for us."

"Not if I help you," she said.

Now it was my turn to gasp. "Really? You would do that, Mom?" I asked, trying not to look too stunned.

"Yes, of course I would. After all that you and Gary have done for me, I would definitely consider helping you buy a home closer to us than what you're talking about. I can sell one of my rental properties and then we can pool our funds and see what we can afford. Maybe you can find something close by. I think that's what you call a win-win, right?"

My head was swimming. As wonderful as this new idea sounded, it made me a little anxious. Bruce and I had been involved in a real estate transaction with my parents many years ago in Hawaii and it had turned out badly for us. It was not my parents' fault; but Bruce and I lost a lot of money. Fortunately, my stepdad was able to recover his investment. My mom had always felt badly about it, and now after all these years, she was telling me that this would be her way to make up for my loss.

"I would like to discuss this with Gary and I want you to talk to Jack about it."

"Of course," she said. "I'll do that when he wakes up from his nap. But let's wait till after the holidays to start the ball rolling. There's just too much going on now and maybe the market will be better in January." I agreed with her. She had always been a very wise businesswoman and I trusted her judgment implicitly when she was as lucid as she was that crisp fall day.

I drove home that afternoon buoyed by the possibility of once again having my own home. I called Gary on his cell phone and discovered that he was already at home. I told him to pick out a really nice cigar and fix me a martini so we could go to the beach immediately and discuss some important news. His curiosity was piqued and he asked me to tell him what was going on. I said no, I wanted to talk with him in person. "You're not pregnant, right?" We both broke into giggles because, at 50, I was already most of the way through menopause and he had had a vasectomy after Cory's birth.

"Did you win the lottery?" he asked.

"No, but I can tell you that it is good news and we can talk about it as soon as I get there."

"Okay," he said. I snapped my cell phone shut.

As I drove up to the house, the garage door was open and Gary was standing there, beach chairs in one hand, my martini in the other, puffing on a big fat cigar. "What are we celebrating?" he asked as I got out of the car.

"C'mon, let's go to the beach and I'll tell you all about it," I replied, taking my martini to free up one of his hands for the cigar.

When we parked our chairs and sat down, I told him about Mom's offer to help with the house. He said he had no problem as long as I was okay with it and it didn't create any more issues with the rest of the family. I assured him it would be fine. I just wanted to be within 10 minutes' drive of their apartment.

Gary agreed with Mom that we should wait until after the first of the year to begin looking at properties. In the meantime, he suggested that I talk with Meg about our plans to be sure she would have plenty of notice and to let her know we would do everything we could to help get a tenant for her. We didn't want her to miss a month of rent on our account.

I was really happy to hear Gary recommend that we talk to Meg, because it was exactly what I wanted to do. Instead of feeling upset about not being able to buy the Lido house, both of us had decided to just let it go because Meg had been so incredibly supportive of our move from the very beginning. For us, the net result had been a closer and more meaningful bond with Meg, Ted and Hannah.

The best part of living close to my parents was being available at a moment's notice if they needed me. This had happened several times in the past eight months. One evening my mom had taken a minor fall while Jack was at the ranch. I had to go over to her apartment to make sure she didn't have any broken bones. Another time, Mom had an infection in a laceration on the back of her thigh which had to be dressed morning and night for several days. I'm not a nurse, but I knew that someone had to do it. So for two weeks after dinner every night, I would drive back to my folks' apartment, clean the wound and put on a new bandage.

Several of my friends asked why we weren't hiring a professional caregiver agency to help with my parents' care. My answer was simply

that my parents did not feel they were ready for
that yet, and I was respecting their wishes. I
would add that if they thought it was easy to
bring in outside caregivers for their parents,
they should read Jacqueline Marcell's book,
*Elder Rage or Take My Father, Please: How to
Survive Caring for Aging Parents.*

I discovered Jaqueline's book on Amazon.
com one day the previous year before we moved
to California. I was searching for books and
resources about caring for aging parents and
this crazy title popped up on my computer
screen. It made me smile. All I needed to do
was substitute the word "Mother" for "Father"
and it perfectly described my feelings.

I ordered the book and when it arrived, I
put it in my briefcase to begin reading on an
upcoming flight from Denver to Orange County.
It turned out to be as informative as it was
funny, a poignant story of a daughter's trials
and learning lessons in becoming a parent to her
parents. Jacqueline went into great detail about
how difficult it was for her parents to accept a
caregiver. Her experience had been similar to
what I was going through. I remember thinking
I needed to try to be the main caregiver for my
parents for as long as I could handle it.

A professional caregiver may have been the
answer for Jacqueline's parents, but an outsider
was not going to cut it with Jack and Marianne.
The one time I tried hiring a company in Newport
Beach to provide care services, Mom fired them
within a couple of weeks. I brought in some other
people to interview and Mom found reasons to
turn each away.

So now that I had assumed the caregiver role, it made sense to live nearby if we could find a way to make it work for us financially. We had to consider the possibility of Mom coming to live with us if something happened to Jack. We needed to find a home that was big enough to accommodate her, too. That was one of the best reasons for letting her help us with the down payment. Gary was adamant that the only way we could bring her to live with us would be to have a house with enough room for her to have an area all to herself, like a small apartment.

We sat on the beach for over an hour that night talking about our plans and about how much we enjoyed living in California. Long after Gary's last puff on the cigar and my last martini olive, we were still sitting and planning and watching the lights out on the bay.

FIFTEEN
HAPPY HOLIDAYS

Only those who have learned the power of sincere and selfless contribution experience life's deepest joy: true fulfillment.

- Anthony Robbins

The holiday season of 2003 was filled with activity. First there was the family Thanksgiving celebration at the ranch hosted by Meg, Ted and Hannah. This was the first time in the past ten years that Gary and I had been able to join everyone for the traditional "over the river and through the woods" trip to the ranch for Thanksgiving. And we had the pleasure of having Cory and Emilie with us, which rounded out the family.

The weather was nice, the turkey was moist, and nobody fell down walking back and forth on the stepping stones over the grassy knolls between the houses. It was great to wake up on the day after Thanksgiving and go shopping in Palm Desert instead of rush into the office to catch up on work that had piled up and needed to be completed before the end of the year. That had been my pattern for way too many holidays.

During the first week in December, Mom was delighted to go shopping for Christmas gifts with me. It was the first time in years that she had been able to go into a store without feeling afraid of falling down or getting lost. We had a wonderful time looking at the lavish decorations at the malls and hearing the sentimental music of the season.

I couldn't recall any holiday season since high school when I had been able to spend so much time shopping, especially with my mom. This year, even if I wasn't buying anything, I suddenly had the luxury of simply looking. Mom told me that taking her out shopping was an integral part of my caregiver job description, and we both laughed. We enjoyed having lunch at Fashion Island and South Coast Plaza, and taking a leisurely afternoon stroll around Balboa Island. She couldn't stay out for too long without becoming tired, so two or three hours were our limit. But two hours of shopping seemed like a lifetime to me, especially when it was every other day for a couple of weeks.

Over the years of working at a full time corporate job, most of my holiday shopping had to be planned out in advance, and then executed very quickly over a few free lunch hours, and never with the spare time to just enjoy looking at the decorations. I was delighted when Internet catalogs started popping up and I could order gifts online late at night in my den or during the lunch hour in my office.

This year, I relished every minute of shopping at malls, boutiques and quaint areas like Laguna Beach. I enjoyed the crowds, the music and the twinkly lights everywhere. There were many baby strollers around during the day and for the first time, I noticed that new moms and babies are ubiquitous at malls. Instead of staying home at my computer in the mornings until my parents were ready for me to come to their apartment, I met girlfriends for coffee at the mall. One of my old friends from Corona del Mar High School, Terry, had recently taken an early retirement from her job and was basking in all her new free time. We had fun comparing notes about being in rehab from the corporate world.

My friends Kathy, Marianne and Vicki had never worked in real corporate jobs. Kathy had been an editor before she was married, Marianne was a golf coach and Vicki was a career domestic goddess. During the years I was working full-time, I used to think it was sad they didn't have careers to balance with their personal lives. Now that I was out of corporate, I could see that their lives were incredibly full and rewarding without a career in business. As I sat in Starbucks with my girlfriends and talked about parents, children, politics and volunteer work, I found myself silently thanking God for letting me see this other side of a life well-lived.

Jack had never liked shopping, even when he could still see. Mom and I both knew that he was feeling left out because we were going out on our little shopping excursions almost every day and he was left alone at the apartment. When we returned from the Lido Isle Women's Club Holiday Luncheon early in December, Jack seemed depressed. He wanted to go to the ranch for the rest of the week, but he couldn't because he had some important doctor's appointments.

I called Meg to tell her Jack seemed to have the holiday blues. Meg suggested we get him busy doing something. She told me when he was at the ranch, she found all kinds of things for him to do, from helping feed the horses to polishing the silver. She took him down to her office in Palm Desert and let him put stamps on envelopes for her business. Best of all, she took him to places where he could share his amazing stories about growing up on the ranch, World War II and owning an aviation company in Orange County. That gave me the idea that he would probably enjoy telling his stories to a tape recorder when he was lonely, and I could transcribe his memories into short stories.

The tape recorder worked for awhile, but Jack still wanted live company. So I planned an excursion with him and Mom to the Braille Institute in Orange. After checking out some books on tape from the friendly staff at Braille Institute, I took my parents to lunch at a little Korean restaurant in Garden Grove. Thankfully, neither one of them could see what they were eating—spicy pickled cabbage, cuttlefish, seasoned rice with a fried egg on top—because if they had been able to see it, they wouldn't have touched anything. But they seemed to enjoy the meal and remarked about how much fun it was to get outside their familiar realm in Newport Beach.

Another day, I got them all dressed up in their Sunday best and we went to a photo session that was offered by their yacht club. As Mom and Jack posed for their portrait, Jack regaled the photographer with stories of being the oldest living yacht club member. Everyone was laughing and the resulting photos, which they gave to the family for Christmas, showed my parents looking happier than we had seen them look in years.

Mom and Jack had been turning down holiday party invitations for the past three years because they were afraid to drive their car after dark and were too proud to call a cab or "impose" on their friends to pick them up. When the first party invitation arrived in the mail, Mom showed it to me and said, "Isn't this a lovely invitation? But of course, we can't go because neither of us can drive."

I looked at the pretty invitation and said, "I don't mind driving you, Mom."

"Oh no, we can't impose on you. You have other things to do in the evening."

"No, really, I would like to take you. Why not go out and socialize if you have the opportunity?" I asked.

She tilted her head sideways and said, "Well, maybe you're right. We could just go for an hour."

"You can go for a couple of hours and you can call me on my cell phone when you're ready to come home," I said.

"That sounds wonderful. I'll call right now and RSVP," she said with a little sparkle in her voice.

This is why I am here, I thought to myself as I listened to Mom leaving a voicemail message accepting the party invitation. My mom has always been a party animal. It must have been awful for her to stay home and miss all the holiday parties and activities the past few years. What fun it was to give that back to her now. This is what my identity is all about today, I said to myself. I'm finally in a position to care – to give something back.

I never would have had the time or the inclination to do this if I was still racking up the ego-driven accomplishments of my brilliant corporate career. Having the time to chauffeur my parents to a few holiday parties made me feel that I was caring for myself by truly demonstrating care and service to others. This heartfelt care and service had sprung from a deep well of respect for my parents' dignity and independence that I had not realized until now.

SIXTEEN
PARTY ON

Nobody cares if you can't dance well. Just get up and dance.

- Dave Barry

Gary and I thrived during the holidays. We found ourselves pinching each other to be sure we were really in Newport Beach with our kids and my extended family. We used to fly from Denver to Palm Springs and drive up to the ranch to spend Christmas with everyone. In 2000, we flew into Orange County to attend a family Christmas celebration at the yacht club before going up to the ranch and the airline lost our luggage with all the gifts. I was so stressed out that I didn't relax until long after the luggage was found and restored to us.

My family had been doing these yacht club Christmas events every year because the little ones loved seeing the holiday boat parade. Hundreds of boats of all types and sizes were covered in colorful lights and decorations ranging from simple strings of lights to extravagant computerized scenes. The glowing boats motored around the harbor in a single line. Homes on the bay front were beautifully adorned in their holiday best for the enjoyment of boat passengers viewing from the water.

I had forgotten all about the boat parade until one night early in December when Gary and I were sitting at the beach. I noticed a large ketch-rigged sailboat across the bay with multicolored strings of Christmas lights outlining its deck, masts and booms. "We'll get to see the boat parade from here," I exclaimed.

"Wow, I hadn't even thought about that," Gary said. "Let's have a party."

With that suggestion and in the tradition of my mother, the great party-giver, I went back to the house and began calling friends to invite them to our home for a walk down to the beach to watch the parade, followed by dinner in front of our fireplace. There were so many people I wanted to invite that we decided to do three parties, including one for our family.

Gary bought a small red wagon and decorated it with a pine garland and white lights, plus a tiny potted Christmas tree with miniature lights and ornaments. "This is our portable cocktail buffet," he said when he wheeled it into the kitchen for me to behold. "You can put your appetizers on the wagon and it will also hold a small cooler and a thermos of hot cider or something." It was adorable and I was delighted by his creative gesture.

I enlisted Mom and Jack to help me plan the party menus. They sampled some of the dishes I prepared in advance, just to be sure I could get the actual dish to look the way it did in the pictures, let alone taste good. I marveled at being able to spend time preparing for a party like this and not having to buy take-out food because I was too busy to cook.

We took digital pictures at each party. The nights were beautiful and we were able to sit on the beach wearing light jackets or sweaters. We stayed out there for over an hour each night, enjoying the enchanting parade and the great camaraderie with our friends and neighbors. Cory, Emilie and Gary couldn't stop talking about being in such perfect weather — a far cry from their previous holidays in Cleveland, Minnesota and Denver. I just smiled and thought I'm genuinely happy to be home again.

Christmas with the family at the ranch was perfect. Cory and Emilie joined Gary and me for five days at my mom's desert condo, a place that was rented for many weeks during the year. We had kept it open for Christmas knowing it would be too tight for the four of us to stay at the ranch with Meg and her family and the folks. We were grateful to have the place to ourselves.

Just two months earlier, I had taken charge of managing Mom's condo rentals from a rental agency in the desert. It was a challenge to figure out how to market the condo. I designed a simple web site and put in some digital photos for people to view. The association had rules about signage so I studied the rules and had a sign made to put up out front. We advertised on a couple of search engines. By far the most inquiries we had were for the week between Christmas and New Year's Day, but we held out to keep it open so our family could stay there. We had a 40-minute commute to the ranch.

The four of us remarked over and over again that this had turned out to be one of our best Christmas celebrations ever. We felt blessed in many ways to be together again, living close to one another, and to be reunited with our extended family and old friends.

Cory and Emilie were also fortunate to have

found a church community not far from their home. Hearing about their church, Gary and I were reminded that we wanted to find a place to nurture our spiritual selves. We knew that the right one was out there somewhere in Orange County, just waiting for us to find it in the New Year. Or maybe it would find us.

SEVENTEEN
A NEW YEAR

There is only one meaning of life; the act of living itself.

- Erich Fromm

On New Year's Eve, Gary, Cory, Emilie and I drove to Pasadena to spend the night at the childhood home of my best friend and cousin, Dru. Dru's main home was in Orange County. She had hung onto her late grandmother's little house in Pasadena because it was located right behind the home of her mom, my Aunt Bettie. Their separate houses shared a backyard fence, making it like a family compound. Aunt Bettie was in her mid-seventies and although still very independent, Dru liked spending time with her. Maintaining her home in Pasadena allowed Dru to be close to her mom, but not too close.

Dru called in early December to ask us to come up for New Year's Eve and then go to the Rose Parade. Her 21 year-old daughter, Shannon, my namesake, would also be coming. Gary and Cory were thrilled because they had always wanted to see the granddaddy of all parades in person.

Dru's daughter, "Little Shannon" was a junior at Long Beach State University. Like our niece, Lindsey, Shannon was very special to us. She and Lindsey were bridesmaids at our wedding in 1999. It was great fun to spend New Year's Eve with her and some of her college friends, as well as Dru and Aunt Bettie. Lindsey and her mom, Nancy, drove over from Glendale to round out our party. We drank champagne and toasted to "La Familia," a fitting end to my year of rediscovery of the deep and profound importance of family and friends.

The Rose Parade did not disappoint, but the rowdy crowd spraying silly string at just about anything that moved was a little hard to take. I mentioned to Gary that I thought most of the revelers were too old to be brandishing silly string cans and he said, "Is anyone ever too old for silly string?" Just then a skinny middle-aged man sprayed string at another guy about the same age, and a fight broke out. Onlookers stopped them from seriously pummeling each other, but couldn't prevent the cowboy's hat from falling off, exposing his very bald head. With silly string hanging off his shiny head and spilling down onto his jacket, he looked more like Bozo the Clown than Clint Eastwood.

As Parade security officers questioned the two silly string marauders, Gary nudged Cory and said, "Aren't you happy you moved to California? It just doesn't get any better than this." Everyone laughed.

After the parade, we had lunch with the gang at a tiny Chinese restaurant. Gary drove the car back to Newport while I dozed in the passenger seat. Listening to the Rose Bowl play-by-play, my mind wandered to New Year's resolutions.

I stopped making resolutions years ago, but this was different. In addition to finding a spiritual home, I wanted to focus on caregiving. Perhaps my experiences could help people whose personal lives had become enmeshed in the pursuit of business and success with little or no time to care for others.

EIGHTEEN
EDUCATION IS THE PROCESS OF DISCOVERY

Whatever relationships you have attracted in your life at this moment, are precisely the ones you need in your life at this moment. There is hidden meaning behind all events, and this hidden meaning is serving your own evolution.
- Deepak Chopra

With the holidays over, my parents and I were back to our normal routine. I went to their apartment every day at noon and stayed till 5p.m., cooking lunch and dinner for them, cleaning house, walking the dog, administering medications and handling finances.

I laughed when I switched to the 2004 pages in my planner and compared this January with the past year. Last January had been filled with client and staff meetings, business trips to Dallas and Houston, prospective client presentations, an ACTE conference steering committee meeting and dozens of conference calls. The 2004 January calendar page held my parents' doctors' appointments, their dog's groomer days, carpet installers at the rental condo in preparation for the sale, Jack's ranch commutes, a cooking class with Emilie and coffee dates with my girlfriends. My life had indeed changed, and at last I was comfortable with it.

One night in mid-January, my friend, Geraldine, called to chat. She was a distant relative of Cousin Dru, who had introduced us a few years ago. She was a professional senior caregiver and had been an invaluable resource during the previous months. Her journey to caregiving was as convoluted as mine. She had lived in Argentina for over 25 years where she had met and married a successful lawyer, had a daughter, Lucia, and eventually divorced. Geraldine owned a wonderful bakery in Buenos Aires, and was a well-known restaurateur. She started a chapter of the Special Olympics in Argentina and relished her active social life.

When Geraldine returned to the US after her divorce, she was disappointed she couldn't find a job that made her heart sing. Crushed by her apparent lack of importance in her new environment, she pressed on. She had discovered that her skills as a cook and years of learning about the hospitality business in Buenos Aires made her an ideal senior caregiver.

When I returned to California, Geraldine had been caring for elderly clients for over five years. I called her for some tips about cooking for people who couldn't be trusted to use the stove or the microwave. She told me to prepare everything in advance, then put it into the microwave, set the proper reheat time, and then just put a big red sticker on the ON button. Even my dad would be able to see the red sticker.

But Geraldine didn't have a life outside of caregiving. She was close to Dru, but Dru was busy with her job as an art professor and other pursuits. Geraldine and I had met for coffee a couple of times and even discussed the possibility of starting our own small caregiver business. But today she was calling to lament her lack of a social life.

"I've made a lot of attempts to be more social here. I even joined a book club, but the members turned out to be authors, and I didn't have much in common with them. One of them even started a kind of New Age breakfast club that meets every week at the University of California, Irvine," she said. "I heard it wasn't a networking organization, but a group that meets to listen to speakers who present all kinds of interesting points of view on what is happening in the world today."

Geraldine's comments about this club instantly sparked my interest. I had to know its name.

"What's the woman's name?" I asked. "I'm going to Google her on the Internet and see if I can find out more about this club because it sounds kind of interesting." I attended UCI and graduated in 1975 and I love going back to the campus, but I hadn't been there since I returned to Newport.

I found the web page for an organization called The Inside Edge.

"That's it," said Geraldine. "I didn't know if it is still in existence."

"It says here the group meets on Wednesday mornings at 6:30. Wow, that's early," I said. "But next week the speaker is Barbara Marx Hubbard. I heard her speak many years ago at a conference in Hawaii and she's wonderful. How about going with me if we can get tickets?"

"You certainly do move quickly, Shannon, but I'm game. I'll go with you this time, and admit I would never go to anything like this by myself."

After we hung up, I read more about The Inside Edge on its web site. The club's vision statement was "Where learning and community come together to nurture your full potential." I loved the idea.

I realized that its next meeting date was also the birthday of my good friend, Marianne, the golf coach, who also enjoyed human potential activities. I called her and told her about the club. "Do you want to get up really early on your birthday and go to this meeting with me?" I asked.

"Sure, why not? It sounds like fun. Thanks for asking me."

NINETEEN
THE INSIDE EDGE

My philosophy is that not only are you responsible
for your life, but doing the best at this moment puts
you in the best place for the next moment.
                              - Oprah Winfrey

The following Wednesday morning, I picked
Marianne up at 6:15 a.m. It was pitch dark
outside and once she was in the car, she said,
"Doesn't it feel strange to be all dressed up at
this hour?" I had to agree, because just an hour
earlier I realized I hadn't worn a business suit
once in the past 10 months. At least my suit still
fit, but my lifestyle had changed so much that I
felt uncomfortable in my "corporate uniform."

When we arrived at the University Club,
Geraldine was already there checking in. Several
smiling men and women literally welcomed us
with open arms. I wondered if Marianne would
be comfortable in what was obviously a touchy-
feely environment, but she was smiling and
hugging strangers enthusiastically.

The three of us were escorted to a table on
the far side of the room. I was surprised to see
about 100 people in the room. At our table,
a tall, attractive middle-aged man stood up to
greet us, shaking our hands. "I'm Jim and I'll
be introducing you as first-timers."

Then he started asking a lot of questions
about each of us and taking notes. I thought
that was a little odd and a bit controlling, but
suddenly I was being asked to stand and Jim

was rattling off my life story in 30 seconds or less.

By the time he was finished introducing all three of us, I was impressed. I thought his "interview" was probably created to keep the introductions short. How many times had I been at a seminar or presentation where the attendees were asked to take a minute to introduce themselves and had taken at least five? This way there was no rambling.

Marianne commented that everyone was way too awake and perky for that hour of the morning. The "regulars" at our table told us they were just used to it. Some of these people had been members of "The Edge" for almost 20 years. The judgment part of my ego wondered if they had anything else going on in their lives.

After the introductions of first-timers, there was a "table talk" where everyone participated in a roundtable discussion about a topic that was introduced by the emcee. I cannot remember the morning's topic, but I know that during the discussion I was able to silence my ego and listen. I marveled at the intelligent, articulate comments made by the others at my table, including my friends. It was as if we were back in college or in a support group at church. Everyone seemed erudite and credible.

During the pre-speaker break, where everyone was supposed walk around and introduce themselves to members, Geraldine pointed out some of the women from her book club, including the founder of "The Edge," Diana Von Welanetz Wentworth. She introduced me to a woman named Kathy who owned a business that supplied plastic bags to The Home Depot. Kathy was nice and I was impressed that she could head up a company doing big business in what was primarily a man's world. Not a day went by that my husband didn't bring home at least one of Kathy's bags.

Another odd thing happened during that break: I found myself wanting to revert to my old way of introducing myself as the vice president of something very important. The truth was I was now a family caregiver, and in this crowd that sounded inconsequential to my ego, which was in a huge battle with my integrity. I struck a pact between the two by blurting out that I was a former marketing executive who had recently moved from Colorado to California to care for my parents. That brought a lot of oohs and ahhs, which satisfied my ego for the moment.

When the break was over and it was time to return to the table, I realized I never made it to the bathroom because so many people had talked with me. This was very much a networking group, even if they didn't admit it. And they were all so bloody happy. I couldn't quite figure out what this group was all about, but I liked it.

Barbara Marx Hubbard was as brilliant and refreshing as she had been when I heard her speak 20 years earlier. She talked about the future and about "Conscious Evolution," which was the title of her latest book. It was a thoughtful and interesting presentation, especially for that hour of the morning.

After a standing ovation for Barbara there was music and another standing ovation. Then it was over and we first-timers were invited to purchase a special "Discovery Member" package that would get us a discounted rate to four of the next six meetings. All three of us bought the package. We agreed that it had been an incredible morning.

Before we left, a very attractive woman about our age in a stunning outfit greeted us warmly. She put her hand out and said, "I just wanted to welcome you. I'm Sandy Moore and it's so nice to see three new faces."

We thanked her.

"My husband, Kirk, is the keyboard player who accompanied the musician. He directs the music for The Edge," she said. "What brought you all here together?"

I told her how I had found the web site, thanks to Geraldine and that it was Marianne's birthday. She smiled again and wished Marianne a great day. Before she could turn and go, I said, "You look familiar, Sandy. Are you from Newport Beach?"

"I work in San Juan Capistrano. I'm a minister. My husband and I have a Religious Science Church called the Center for Universal Truth."

My jaw dropped.

"Really?" I said. "I used to go to the Huntington Beach Church and then I went to the Mile Hi Church in Denver for 10 years."

"So you know Roger Teel!" she exclaimed, her eyes widening.

"Yes, I knew him here when he was assistant minister at Huntington Beach, and then he came back to Denver," I said.

"We're doing some things now to model successful programs that Mile Hi has created," she said. "Why don't you come to one of our services sometime, if it's not too far for you? Pick up one of our brochures on the back table here before you leave."

"I'll do that," I said.

It was magical. I had never been to Sandy's church; or even looked at the brochure. Yet I knew then and there that I had found a very special spiritual home for Gary and me. Or maybe it had found me, because I was open and ready to experience this brief, heartfelt connection of kindred spirits.

My intuition momentarily took my breath away while I realized this encounter was a gift to treasure and share. I vowed to visit the Center for Universal Truth very soon.

Before leaving, we were invited to join a group that met at a nearby Starbucks afterwards for coffee and conversation. I wanted to go and Geraldine said she would follow me.

There were about 20 people sitting around some tables that had been pushed together. I only recognized Jim, the fellow who had introduced us. Yet all of them were motioning for us to join them.

This was the nicest, most interesting group of strangers I had ever met. They asked questions and listened to answers. They offered advice to one another if asked. Best of all, they laughed a lot. I left Starbucks feeling more invigorated than I had felt in years. If this group is always this way, I've discovered something better and cheaper than therapy. And of course my ego voice whined that this group was composed of wackos in need of therapy. *Look in the mirror, Ego Bitch.*

I couldn't wait for the next meeting.

TWENTY
ONE STEP BACK

No problem is too big to run away from.
- Charles Schultz

As if that day had not been exciting enough already, when I got home and was changing back into my ubiquitous sweats, the phone rang. It was my mom's realtor, Lisa.

"Your mom called and told me that she wants to list her beach condo and that you and Gary are going to buy a house with her," she said. "She wants me to come over this afternoon with the listing papers."

I was shocked. Mom and I hadn't discussed the plan to buy a house since before the holidays, but I was also delighted.

"I was hoping that I could come to your house on Lido this afternoon because I have to be over there to show some property. Your mom said that she might be over there with you anyway."

"Yes, that's fine," I said. Jack was at the ranch and it was easy to bring Mom to our house.

The condo was vacant. The previous tenants had moved out in November. Gary and Cory had just finished painting and fixing or replacing some faulty old appliances. While they worked on it, Mom asked us to seriously consider moving into it; but we wanted a house, not a condominium. We needed a backyard for Vanna and a driveway where Gary could work on his beloved old cars. He was itching to buy an old Mustang and a driveway was a key element for his project.

Lisa's company was showing the vacant condo to potential renters during the month of January. Lisa, Gary or I had been going up to check on it every two or three days to be sure that smoke alarms weren't chirping and lights were turned off. We were glad the place had not been rented because we wouldn't have to ask a tenant to vacate when it sold.

Mom signed the listing and Lisa said it would go into multiple listings the next week. Unfortunately, two days later we discovered the downstairs area was completely flooded. We called the Homeowners Association and they brought in a plumber who discovered a serious slab leak. Hot water was pouring into the unit from underground.

The damage was extensive. I spent the entire day with the plumber and the damage recovery company. The president of the Homeowners Association Board of Directors dropped by to inspect the disastrous mess.

There was no way we could get the place cleaned up and put back together in a few days. Mold had already started to grow on the baseboards in the downstairs bedroom where the new carpet was completely soaked. I called Lisa and told her to hold off on the listing.

Things only got worse because the condo management company insisted on using their preferred vendor for the repairs. The uncooperative vendor said he could not do the repairs for at least three weeks. I was livid, but didn't want to go against the Association's wishes because if we did, we'd have to pay for the repairs ourselves.

Meanwhile, Lisa had already lined up places for Mom, Gary and I to look at in Costa Mesa. I debated about whether we should see any of them because any house purchase was contingent on the condo selling. The real estate market was still hot and properties were going very fast, sometimes even before they hit the multiple listing service.

Lisa convinced us to take a look. I fell in love with the very first home we saw. It was a wonderful old Costa Mesa bungalow that had been remodeled with a modern kitchen with granite countertops and stainless steel appliances. Lisa took the wind out of my sails right away by saying that the seller was expecting at least four offers that afternoon.

Over the next few days, we looked at other properties. The only constant was that they were all sold before we saw them. This frustration on top of the slab leak fallout was testing my ability to stay positive and believe everything was happening for a reason.

On Valentine's Day, Geraldine called to ask if we were still looking for a home in Costa Mesa. I told her we were.

"Remember I told you I sometimes baby-sit for my friend's daughter who has a toddler? Well, she called to see if I could take care of the baby tonight. And she also told me they're going to put their home on the market soon because they bought a big new house in Newport," she said.

"Where is the house?" I asked.

"It's in a wonderful neighborhood and it's on a corner lot," she said. She gave me the address and told me to drive by and if we liked it, we could call their realtor and set up a time to see it.

We went to see the property the next day. It was everything we wanted in a home, on a huge lot with beautiful, blooming white rosebushes all around the perimeter. Large pine trees lined the quiet street and reminded us of Colorado. There was a quaint patio, a very large backyard, and a big garage for Gary. The house needed some work, but Gary was a contractor up to the task. Even Mom liked it. There was room for a mother-in-law suite if we needed one. We knew it was the perfect home for us.

Although the house wasn't listed yet, I overheard the owner's realtor tell Lisa that he was expecting a couple of offers by the next day. Instead of being discouraged, I was sure we were not going to lose our dream home. There was too much synchronicity in the way we found it and how perfect it was for our needs.

We went back to the house on Lido Isle and plotted how we could list the condo even with the walls opened up and the floors torn apart. I knew that we were meant to have the little house surrounded by roses. It was just a matter of making it happen.

TWENTY-ONE
THERE ARE ALWAYS CHALLENGES

Accept the challenges so that you may feel the exhilaration of victory.
                    - General George S. Patton

Just as we found our dream house, Lisa had to go out of town, so she asked us to work with her associate, Rita, who helped us put together an offer. Rita was very competent and, best of all she didn't think that I was crazy to believe that we could get this house.

Rita arranged a showing of the condo for the weekend and, lo and behold we received offers that were more than we were asking, even with the slab leak mess. But my excitement about the multiple offers subsided when the first offer we accepted fell through the next day, followed by the second one. Apparently there was a lawsuit against the Homeowners Association for a mold problem on another unit affecting our sale.

I hadn't paid attention to mold issues in the housing industry until this happened. After we lost the second sale, my Internet research revealed mold was creating huge problems all over the country. I became concerned about the possibility of mold in our unit due to the delay in the slab leak repairs. But I decided to focus on something positive and constantly remind myself that this transaction was destined to happen.

Unfortunately after four days we still hadn't heard back from the sellers of the Costa Mesa house. Their realtor indicated though we had bid above the asking price, we might be too low. We were very upset, but I didn't lose hope.

A week after our offer had been submitted, my cell phone rang while I was making my parents' lunch.

"Are you sitting down?" It was Rita.

"No."

"They have accepted your offer," she said. I was yelling "YES" and jumping up and down in the kitchen, holding my cell phone and half of a turkey sandwich. Mom and Jack knew then that it was Rita calling with good news.

I called Gary to tell him we were now on the home stretch. He was elated. Ever since we had seen the house for the first time, he had been saying, "The house is ours." His reaction was so strong it built on my feeling that this was where we were meant to be. It was February 27th, our fifth wedding anniversary and exactly one year from the day we started our new life in Southern California.

The next day we heard that the third offer on the condo was secure. However, the buyers wanted to have a mold inspection. Alarm bells went off in my mind and I did everything I could to reverse my negative emotions.

The inspection showed that the mold in the condo was so bad it was "off the charts." To make matters worse, the construction crew from the damage recovery company had sealed up the walls without treating the mold.

After receiving the inspection report, I called a meeting of the management company, the damage recovery team, the buyer and his realtor and Rita and Lisa. I emailed everyone an agenda and felt like I was back in the corporate world. The meeting did not go well. It became very clear we would have to proceed with mold remediation and reconstruction at our own expense to meet the buyer's requirements. Still, my top priority was to make it through our escrow for the Costa Mesa house. And I knew we would have to pay for the damage repair if that was our only path.

The buyer of the condominium was very nice. His realtor was also his mother. She referred me to a mold remediation company that she had used, and gave me the contact information for the inspector. Once all the work was done, the inspector would give the go-ahead in order for the buyer to proceed.

That night I did not sleep at all. It was really hard to keep the faith under such tense circumstances. I had no idea how Gary and I were going to pay for the quick mold remediation. Mom would have waited patiently for the condo association management company to get the repairs completed at their expense. We couldn't risk losing our dream home, so we felt obligated to pay for the speedy remediation. Thankfully Mom was a good sport in supporting our desire to get the house we wanted.

Someone once told me that anger is like taking poison and waiting for the other person to die; I forgot about that in the wake of the mold debacle. When I told Gary that I was angry and suffering from insomnia, he suggested I "get over it." My anger and fear wasn't going to resolve the issues. So I began balancing these negative feelings of anger and worry with lots of deep breathing and meditating every day. I kept visualizing living in the house and having lunch on the peaceful garden patio in the backyard.

Every day there were more problems. The remediation process was long and we had to propose a delay in the close of escrow for the Costa Mesa house. Thankfully, the sellers accepted the delay, but we had to agree to pay a very large per diem that amounted to about $10,000 added to the purchase price.

I kept my chin up. I went to The Inside Edge meetings every week and took great pleasure in the inspiring messages and new friends I was making.

And something else happened that made us believe that fate was on our side. Cory and Emilie came up to Newport to go to dinner with us one night in March and asked us if we could keep a secret for a couple of months. We said yes, of course, although keeping any kind of secret is always a huge challenge for me.

"We have some good news," Cory said. "Emilie is pregnant." Gary and I were stunned for a few seconds and could only say, "Wow, that's wonderful." And then Gary's eyes filled with tears, which triggered the same reaction in me. We were overcome with joy because our children lived nearby and now we could share in the gift of creating a new human life. Without ever giving birth to a child of my own, I was going to experience the miracle of grand-parenting. I remember saying to Cory, Emilie and Gary, "When we think our lives are full of challenges, something happens that reminds us it just doesn't get any better than this. We have to have faith."

TWENTY-TWO
MORE SIGNS

The higher order of logic and understanding that is capable of meaningfully reflecting the soul comes from the heart.

- Gary Zukav

One night in the middle of the escrow period I was having trouble sleeping, so I checked out The Inside Edge web site to see who some of the past speakers were. I had already discovered that The Edge advisory board included some of the people I most admired: Dr. Wayne Dyer, Louise L. Hay, Jack Canfield, Mark Victor Hansen, Terry Cole Whittaker, Jean Houston and Barbara De Angelis, among others.

As I reviewed some of the past speakers, I saw another familiar name: Jacqueline Marcell. There was a video of her talk in The Edge library online, as well as a link to her own web site. I clicked on the link and went to her list of upcoming presentations. Coincidentally, she was scheduled to appear at Orange Coast College in Costa Mesa the very next week.

I didn't want to make a lot of noise with the printer right then because Gary was sleeping, so I bookmarked the page to print it later. I felt this was a sign. The comfort of knowing that I had again discovered a positive sign helped me get a few hours sleep without thinking about the house drama.

When the night arrived, Geraldine and I drove together to Orange Coast College to see

Jacqueline's talk. We sat in the front row.

Jacqueline turned out to be a delightful speaker. She shared important information about caring for elderly parents, and she was funny. In a poignant moment, she told the group her parents had passed away recently.

Afterwards, Geraldine and I went up to the stage and spent a few minutes talking with her. I told her how much I had enjoyed her book and had used the resources she listed. She said to feel free to email her any time for more information. I was impressed by her down-to-earth personality, innate kindness and sense of humor.

Something about meeting Jacqueline that night inspired me to think that perhaps I could write a book about caring for my own parents, but from a different perspective than hers. My focus was how caring for my parents was teaching me invaluable lessons about how to respect and care for myself.

My career and the money I made had been so important that I had refused to move from Hawaii to California with Bruce in 1986. I had been okay with letting our marriage flounder for two years. I decided not to have children because I didn't want to leave my job for several months of bed rest. Worst of all, I had let a friend down when she was dying of cancer because I was too busy with work projects to make the time to spend with her.

As I got further away from the corporate world, I noticed how painfully difficult it had been for me to balance business with my personal life. More often than not during my years in the corporate environment, I had made business goals a priority over personal development and relationships. Reflecting on that long period of my life, I was disappointed to think that I had chosen business over pleasure so many times. It seemed as if business was the only pleasure for me during those hectic years.

Choosing to let go of business and embrace caring for my parents had shown me the way to care for myself. I knew after Jacqueline's talk that my career in business was not over, but my purpose now included helping people find balance — helping nurture themselves as well as their careers in Corporate America. I had no idea how that purpose would play out. My ego voice screamed that I was not competent to do such a thing and had no business declaring such a lofty purpose.

Thank you for sharing, I said to myself. *Stop criticizing and second-guessing yourself and let something bigger than your ego show you the way.* That was all the conversation I needed. I slept well for the first time in several days.

TWENTY-THREE
Believe and Let It Unfold

I am open to the guidance of synchronicity and do not let expectations hinder my path.
- Dalai Lama

By the middle of April, we still had not completed the purchase of our new home, but no matter how many obstacles were thrown in our path we didn't give up. Gary and I believed we were meant to live in the house, so we did everything we could to make it happen, including prayers and visualizations. We also enjoyed some diversions.

Our dear friends from Denver, Michael and LuAnn, came to California for a long weekend with us at the beach. Michael rented a funny little Duffy electric boat and we toured Newport Harbor, then went out to a fancy restaurant for cocktails and dinner by the bay. By the time they left, Gary and I felt as if we had been on a weekend vacation too.

On Easter Sunday, we took my parents to the *Alice in Wonderland* Easter Brunch at the Disneyland Hotel. We were joined by Meg and her family, Cory and Emilie and Emilie's parents who were visiting from Minnesota. It was a brunch beyond everyone's wildest dreams. At Disneyland, you don't get anything as mundane as an "omelet man," you're treated to big fresh strawberries dipped in an endless milk chocolate fountain and enormous carved chocolate sculptures featuring Disney characters. Mom and Jack had fun too.

I was delighted that some of the hotel banquet staff remembered me. It made me feel great to know that I could come back 10 years later and talk with acquaintances who were still working there. Sharing with them that Gary and I had moved to California so I could care for my parents made me feel whole.

The weekend after Easter, we decided to go to Sandy Moore's church, The Center for Universal Truth, for the first time. It was located in San Juan Capistrano, a pretty little town in South Orange County. The town was built around the old Mission San Juan Capistrano, founded by Father Junipero Serra in 1775. This particular mission is famous for the swallows, tiny birds that return to nest every spring, usually on the same day. I liked the idea of attending a church that was in this wonderful, historic town.

While I was online looking at the Center For Universal Truth web site, I noticed a mention of the reopening of the Tara's Angels Bookstore at the Center. I was curious about it, so I clicked on the link, which took me to an information page about Sandy and Kirk Moore. Their daughter, Tara, had been killed in a tragic car accident in 1994; that very night she began contacting them from her new realm among the angels.

The story gave me goose bumps because it made me think about my communications with Bruce, my father and grandmother. I noted that Kirk Moore had written a book called *Tara's Angels*, and that his family had been featured in *People Magazine* and on a national television program about angels. I had another eerie sensation that I was on the right path, but I didn't want to share it with Gary because I thought he might think me crazy.

So the next day we went to church. As much as I sometimes think Gary is more skeptical than I am, if the message is right and the moment is magical, he is often more open to divine experiences than I am. As we sat and listened to the music before the service, he squeezed my hand and when I looked at him, he said, "At last, we're home." And I knew he was right.

One of the first things I noticed about Sandy was her gift of communicating to the entire congregation as if she was talking to each of us individually. Her message went straight to my heart. She was inspiring, funny and very real. I had the same kind of extraordinarily positive experience listening to a Sunday message that I had when attending services by Dr. Roger Teel at Mile Hi Church and Dr. Peggy Bassett at HBCRS.

Gary and I talked about the service on the way home. We agreed Sandy had an amazing ability to communicate. We wondered why the congregation was so small, given that she was so good. "Perhaps she was better today than she usually is," Gary said. "Let's see how it is next week."

That was good news, because Gary was telling me that he wanted to go back, which meant that I wouldn't have to beg him to go with me the following Sunday. I was happy this wasn't the fall season when church services would compete with football, because football would win. But

more importantly, I felt that attending this little
church in San Juan Capistrano was somehow
connected to our closing escrow on our home in
Costa Mesa. I had no idea why, but it was as if
attending this church was part of the miracle of
my journey back home. I just had to follow my
intuition and believe.

The next day Lisa called to say that we had
big problems with closing the sale on the condo.
I told her that we would do whatever we needed
to do to satisfy the buyers, even if it meant a
financial concession. And we would also have
to find a way to coax the sellers of the Costa
Mesa house to agree to another delay for the
escrow closing. We knew it would be costly.
But we also knew that it would all work out in
our favor.

The following Sunday, we went back to the
Center for Universal Truth. Kirk's music was
lively and Sandy shared another marvelous
message that felt like it was just for Gary and
me. After the service, I filled out a prayer request
form and asked for support in closing escrow on
both the sale of the condo and the purchase of
the Costa Mesa home.

Five days later, not without some requisite
last-minute drama, both the escrows closed. We
had hopes of recovering some of the money we
had spent to correct the problems that resulted
from the slab leak. We didn't need to pay an
exorbitant amount to delay closing on the Costa
Mesa house after all. Nevertheless, the ordeal
had been enough to test our resiliency and faith.
In the end, we had let synchronicity and faith
guide us and keep us on the path.

Geraldine's Valentine prediction that Gary and I were meant to live in the little old house in Costa Mesa with the rose bushes and pine trees in the front yard had finally come true. And now, because of the delays in closing escrow, we had only 12 days to get our new little home fixed up so that we could vacate the Lido house in time for the new renter.

TWENTY-FOUR
OH, YE OF LITTLE FAITH

Release it to the Universe.
- Gary Ingram

It was around 4:30 p.m. on escrow closing day when we got the keys to our new home. We picked up Mom and Jack and then stopped by the liquor store and bought a bottle of Veuve Clicquot champagne. I had put four champagne flutes and four folding chairs into the car earlier in the day in hopes of a celebration.

Once we were inside our new little house and Gary had set up the chairs and seated the folks, I opened the champagne and we all shared a toast to our good fortune. Within seconds, Gary was in the back room knocking down walls with a big sledge hammer. "I don't have any time to waste," he said, and I knew he was right.

We had major renovations to complete — transforming a small studio apartment in the back of the house into a master suite, refinishing all the wood floors, removing some ancient floor heaters, electrical work, and making new hallway access to the master bedroom. It was like the television program, *Extreme Makeover: Home Edition*, only without the army of helpers, design team and unlimited budget. Fortunately, we had Gary and his general contracting company, and he assured me that he could get the job done by the time the movers arrived.

Gary was so obsessed with his renovation and demo work that Mom suggested I drive

them home and celebrate some other night. I
was a little disappointed, but I knew that Gary
had every minute planned and tonight's planned
minutes didn't include dinner at Mi Casa.

When I returned to the house after dropping
off Mom and Jack and making sure they had
something to eat for dinner, I found Cory and
Emilie there too. They were thrilled for us,
and Cory was pitching in with the demolition.
I ordered pizza and salad to feed our pregnant
Emilie and the demo boys. By 10p.m., Gary and
Cory had torn cabinets out and removed carpet
torn from the floor in the back room.

The next few days were filled with activity
and difficulties galore. Because of our escrow
extension, we would not have Cory to help. He
and Emilie had planned a trip to Florida. By the
third day, Gary was working too hard without
help and the strain was showing. I asked him
to take a break, but he blew me off and told me
to go back home to Lido and continue packing.
That's when I blew up.

"You can't do all this yourself and I won't
stand idly by and watch you have a heart
attack or a stroke," I yelled at him. I picked up
a chunk of wood and threw it against the wall
for dramatic effect. I made it more theatrical by
getting a big, fat splinter in my middle finger in
the process.

"Ouch," I muttered, spitting out the word
and pinching my finger. I tried to get the splinter
to pop out but it was well-imbedded beneath my
skin. I could hear Gary chuckling across the
room. Another argument had been diffused by
my clumsiness.

"Okay, I'll hire a couple of guys to help me, but that will drive our costs up and I've been trying to save money because we spent so much on the escrow delay," he said. "Now get out of here before you really hurt yourself."

I had to laugh. I felt like a character in a *Far Side* cartoon I had seen years earlier. It was a skinny guy in a furry suit that was part of some kind of a Viking rowing crew on a boat. He had stopped rowing and his hand was up in the air to get the attention of a big burly man at the front of the boat dressed in horns and chains and holding a whip. The caption was "Excuse me but I think I have a splinter."

"I wish I could help you here, Gary, but I know I'm out of my realm, so I quietly and with dignity accept your invitation to leave." I chuckled.

He smiled and said, "Release it to the universe, Shannon. Everything will turn out fine." I flipped my splinter finger at him, turned around and walked to my car. That was around 6p.m.. Gary didn't come home until well after midnight.

The next day when I drove over to the new house with some boxes, Gary was there along with two other men. He introduced them and said they would be working for us until the job was completed. I couldn't stop the control freak in me from blurting out, "I guess that will be May 26th because that's the day we move in."

"Yes, and thank you for sharing," Gary replied.

My good friend, Terry, who, by cosmic fortune lived diagonally across the street from our new home, came over that afternoon to check on our progress. When she saw the mess in the back room, she gasped and said, "I don't know, Shannon. Do you really think you can move in here next week?"

"We have to move, so my answer is yes. If we have to live in the front part of the house for awhile, we will do that," I said. But I was thinking about the mess in the front of the house too. There was a gaping hole in a living room wall. The first day of demo, Cory was really excited and asked me if I was planning to redo the kitchen and take the wall down. I said yes and before I could add, "in a few months," he raised his sledgehammer and slammed it into the drywall. "ARGHHHH," I screamed. "Not now!" But it was too late.

Rather than get all worked up about the hole, I decided that we could put a temporary window into the kitchen until we decided to do the second stage remodel. Now, as I was standing there with Terry in the midst of the mess, she noticed the newly framed "window."

"Hey," she said. "Why don't we make it into a puppet show window?" I cracked up. And on that note, we walked over to her house for a glass of wine.

I was not making very fast progress packing and we had only five days till the move. Gary said it was his turn to make a suggestion. "Why don't you see what it would cost to have the movers do the rest of the packing?"

"I have never had anyone pack my stuff unless it was being paid for as part of a transfer package," I said.

"Well, you don't have a transfer package now, do you? And you don't have anyone helping you to pack, and you're stressed out about all that has to be done, right?"

"Yes."

"Well, then, call the movers and ask them about packing."

That turned out to be the best suggestion Gary ever made. The fee was reasonable so I surrendered and hired them to come the day before the move and do the rest of the packing. It was pretty easy. Jack offered to come over and sit at the house while the movers packed, which was great because I had to leave and take Mom to a previously scheduled doctor's appointment. He hung out with the packers for part of the day and entertained them with stories about the ranch. A good time was had by all.

That evening when the packing crew departed, I drove Jack home and fixed dinner for him and Mom. Then I went to the house to see how Gary was doing in preparation for the next day's move. The past few days had been a disaster because the floors were being refinished, and although he had an army of helpers completing the drywall, electrical and painting that evening, the place was still a mess. I sat down on a folding chair on the front lawn and cried, mostly because nobody wanted to hear about my concerns or share any of my misery.

"Oh ye of little faith," Gary said. "I told you we'd be ready tomorrow, and we shall be ready. Please stop crying and focus on something good." Once again, Gary had found the right words to snap me out of my personal pity party. Then he gave me a big, sweaty hug.

I drove home to Lido and parked on the street because the garage was full of boxes. I went into the living room and sat down on the sofa. Poudre and Vanna jumped up onto the cushions next to me, something they never do, especially together. I figured they were rightly agitated because of all the upheaval. I told my pets, "Everything is going to be all right. Have faith," but of course I was really saying it to myself.

When Gary got home around midnight, I was asleep on the sofa. "Did you finish?" I asked him.

"No, we have a little more painting to do and some clean-up, but we'll be ready for your movers when they arrive."

I was too tired to worry. And besides, I thought, what good does it do to worry? Worry is a prayer for the thing you fear to happen. So all I said in response to Gary's comment was, "I have faith."

TWENTY-FIVE
TRUST THE DANCE

They sicken of the calm that know the storm.
- Dorothy Parker

One of my teachers, Marshall Thurber, said there are times in life when you have to trust the dance. I think of Gary's "Release it to the universe" as a variation on the same theme. My experience of buying and moving into the house in Costa Mesa was all about trusting the dance. Whenever my trust level dropped and I succumbed to worry or had a breakdown in the midst of chaos, I always told myself to trust the dance.

The bad news was that house was not ready on the morning of our move. The good news was that the movers did not finish loading the truck at the Lido house until around 2p.m. By the time I arrived in Costa Mesa with the moving van, Gary and his crew had worked a miracle: they had cleaned up everything and we were able to move all the furniture and boxes inside, taking care not to damage the wet paint on the living room walls.

We went to dinner at Mi Casa with Mom and Jack because I hadn't been able to prepare a meal for them that day. We felt like celebrating with Mexican food.

As I lay in bed that night looking up at the skylight in my new bedroom, I thought about the many challenges Gary and I had overcome in the past year, and particularly in the past

two weeks. In my heart, I knew everything
would eventually turn out all right, but so
many obstacles had been thrown in our path.
Looking back on the past few months, I realized
there were many times when I got caught up in
a storm and had a hard time letting go of it. For
me, there is something attractive and familiar
about turbulent times. As the child of a broken
home, I grew up in a challenging, albeit loving,
environment. That night I wondered if I was
subconsciously re-creating turbulence because
it fed my spirit.

We had a blissful time getting our new
home organized during the next few weeks. We
bought an ornate Florentine fountain for the
back patio and Gary installed it in a perfect
spot just outside my office window. We put up
shelves in my office. Gary built a wonderful
front porch we could sit on and enjoy watching
the summer activity on the street. We brought
Mom and Jack over at least once a week for
dinner so they could enjoy keeping up with the
progress.

Things were going so well that we decided
to plan a party for the end of July. We invited
Sandy and Kirk, our ministers, and two other
couples from our church. I tested barbecue
recipes out on Mom and Jack again and we
chose a tri-tip with some tasty side dishes.
Again I had that sense of being very far removed
from my life in the corporate world, only this
time I was grounded in being a homemaker and
caregiver.

The day of the party arrived and I was
delighted that preparations were going smoothly.

I was able to spend a few hours with Mom and Jack, which was important because they had come to depend on our time together. I left their apartment around 3:30p.m.

The meat had been marinating overnight. The garlic potatoes had been par-boiled and were wrapped in foil ready to throw on the barbie. The patio tables were set and the wine was chilled. Gary arrived home at 4 p.m. and said he would be cleaning up his garage a bit so that he could show it off as his "cigar bar," complete with cable TV. Our guests were due to arrive at 6p.m.

I was preparing salad vegetables when the phone rang at 5. I checked the caller i.d. and noticed it was Mom's phone number. I picked up the phone and said hello, feeling mildly irritated that they would call me knowing I was really busy.

"Shan, I am so sorry to bother you, but Jack was taking a nap and I heard a loud crash and a moan. I ran into his room and he had fallen out of bed and his television fell on top of him and now his head is bleeding and he's not making any sense."

"Call 911, Mom, right now," I said, feeling panic creeping into my calm demeanor.

"He won't let me call 911," she said. "I want you to come over and then you can call 911."

By this time I had walked out to the garage with the phone and was now standing in front of Gary who knew something was wrong.

"Hold on, Mom, let me tell Gary what's happening." Gary had a background in forensic pathology, and although that did not qualify him as a doctor, he knew a lot about symptoms and medical conditions.

"It sounds as if he may have had a stroke," Gary said. "I'll head over there and call 911 from my cell right now. I should get there at the same time the paramedics do. You stay here and turn off all the appliances. I will call and let you know how serious it is and then you may have to meet us at the hospital. I'm guessing you'll need to call the guests and cancel the party."

I shared his comments with Mom and she said okay before breaking into sobs. Gary had already left in his truck.

"Mom, you need to hold it together right now. Just go sit with Jack and wait for Gary and the paramedics to get there."

"I'm so sorry about your dinner party," she said.

"That's the least of our worries. I'll come as soon as I can, and Gary should be there any minute now. I'll stay on the phone with you, or I can hang up and call your neighbors, Jim and Kathy, if you want me to."

"No, please stay on the phone," she said. I can hear the sirens." She was starting to cry again. "Jack is talking gibberish. I gave him some paper towels for his head, but he won't use them. And there is blood all over the floor."

"Why don't you try and clean up his head?" I asked.

"Here's Gary, so I can go now," she said. The phone just clicked off.

Gary called me within seconds to say the paramedics were there and they would stabilize Jack before taking him to the hospital. I told him that I was making phone calls and would meet them in the ER.

I was able to reach two of the couples to deliver the bad news, but I had to leave a message for Sandy and Kirk. I knew they were at a wedding rehearsal somewhere and probably had their cell phones off. I left a note on the door for them in case they arrived to find no one home.

As I was leaving the house, Gary called to say that the ambulance had just left for the hospital with Mom riding in the front seat, and he was going to drive there in his truck.

"I'm on my way to meet you," I said, and hung up.

I had to smile at the thought of my mom riding shotgun in an ambulance down Pacific Coast Highway at rush hour on a Friday. I felt certain that it would take her mind off the crisis for a few minutes.

The paramedics were wheeling Jack into the Emergency Room when I arrived at the parking lot. I saw one of them help Mom out of the front seat and she looked as if she was in shock walking behind the gurney. Mom started to cry when she saw me.

"Hey, it's going to be ok," I said, trying to sound soothing as I hugged her. "How was the ride in the ambulance?"

Her facial expression morphed immediately from sadness and fear to amazement. "It was really great. I got to sit in the front next to Charlie, the driver. Charlie told me I was in for a wild ride and it sure was. We went on the wrong side of the highway for awhile with the siren blaring.

I kind of wished that one of my friends could see me, but then I thought they might have worried about why I was in the ambulance."

I had to giggle because she really was excited. The nurses were hooking Jack up to the monitors and one of them asked me to review and sign some papers. I turned to Jack and said, "How are you doing, Jack?" He stuttered, "What dddddo you think?"

"You don't look too good with that big gash on your head."

"I fell out of bed and broke my head," he said without missing a syllable. "But I think I'm sick."

"We'll find out soon enough," I replied.

"I'm sorry that we ruined your party," Mom said.

"There will be other parties," I said.

At that moment, Gary walked in. "How ya doin, Jack-o?" he asked.

Jack just raised his hand as if to say so-so, but nothing came out of his mouth. "Sandy just called to say they were running a little behind after the wedding rehearsal. I told them what's happening with Jack and they offered prayers and asked for us to call if we needed anything," he said.

Gary stayed for about 10 minutes and then we sent him home because there were too many of us around the bed. He promised to call Meg and Ted and let them know about Jack's condition and I would supply him with updates.

Meg, Ted and Hannah arrived at 7. They had been in Del Mar for a long weekend holiday.

Jack was glad to see them and, although he had trouble finding words, he even managed to crack a joke.

After hours of tests punctuated by long periods of just sitting and watching the wavy lines on the monitors, the ER doctor finally told us that Jack had indeed suffered a stroke. The doctor said he would admit Jack into the hospital and Jack's regular doctor had called a specialist who would see him "later." I asked when he would be admitted and they said, "as soon as possible." It was 9:30 p.m.

Mom was exhausted. Meg suggested I take her home while she stayed at the hospital with Jack. Hannah and Ted were spending the evening in the waiting room watching television. I asked if she wanted me to come back and she said, "I don't think so. They're just going to take him to a room, right?" I nodded, and thankfully, Mom didn't resist leaving.

TWENTY-SIX
DECISIONS, DECISIONS

Decisions, particularly important ones, have always made me sleepy, perhaps because I know that I will have to make them by instinct, and thinking things out is only what other people tell me I should do.
- Lillian Hellman

The next few days after Jack's stroke were hectic with each of the family members taking turns spending time at the hospital. He was improving a little and didn't have any catastrophic side effects. His speech was slow and slurred, but we could understand most of what he was communicating. He had a little weakness on his left side, but he could walk with a walker or cane.

On Sunday night, I served the food that I had planned and prepared for my cancelled party to my family members who had gathered at our home. We had just enough for everyone and the meal was pretty good although my heart was not into entertaining.

Meg and I were dismayed to find a note on the door of Mom and Jack's apartment from the night before saying that they would have to vacate the premises in one week and be out for up to six weeks. The management company was taking care of some serious problems. We had known since March this was imminent; but we had not predicted Jack's illness.

The doctors told us Jack would not be released into a skilled nursing facility because he didn't need that level of care. They said he would require round-the-clock care for several weeks while recovering at home.

I had researched home care agencies in the past year just in case. I had selected an agency with a good reputation. One of the women who worked at the agency was a regular at The Inside Edge, so I called to give her a heads-up that we would need a caregiver. She promised they could mobilize support for us with very little notice. That afternoon she sent someone to Mom and Jack's apartment to check it out and make recommendations.

Now, on top of everything else, we were faced with moving my parents within a week. I called the apartment management office to see if we could delay their "temporary move to another unit" for a couple of months and was told no. I knew we would have to figure something out because there was no way that we could move Mom and Jack twice in the next two months.

We needed a quick but lasting "fix." Our parents would absolutely and flatly refuse to move to an assisted living facility. We had been down that road with them several times in the past few years.

During the family dinner at our home Sunday evening, Meg and I decided that our best course of action was to find another two-bedroom unit in the "pet section" of the complex that had already been remodeled. Somehow, I knew we would find one. The big challenge would be moving them on one week's notice with Jack just out of the hospital.

After the dishes were done and everyone

had gone home, I sat down in the living room with Gary. "Everything had been going so well since we moved into this house," I said. "And now, this happens. Jack will require a great deal more attention when he gets out of the hospital than he has needed in the past. I simply cannot do that, and I don't want to do it any more. It's too draining."

"I agree," Gary said. "Why don't you take the next few days before Jack gets home and think about doing something else. Why don't you write a book? You've been talking about that for years. Or you could do some consulting."

"Maybe it's time for me to get a corporate job," I said. "We've been doing okay financially with your job and my gift from Mom; but I can't accept money from her now that they have to pay for round-the-clock caregivers."

"I understand," Gary said. "You'll have to decide if you want another desk job somewhere, but I know you have enjoyed having a flexible schedule this past year. You said you'd love to work from your office here at home, so why not try that?"

I am afraid, I thought, but said nothing.

When I had my own business in Hawaii years earlier, it had been very hard for me. I loved doing the writing and public relations projects, but I hated the accounting and collecting money from clients. I got out after only one year. I was only 35 then, and now I was much wiser and had more tools to make it easier to be a freelancer.

"I know I have to do something," I said. "But I want to wait till after our Mexico cruise in

September because if I start a job any earlier, we might have to cancel."

"We will not cancel the cruise," said Gary in his most emphatic and commanding tone of voice. "We have not had a vacation in two years and we need this one."

"Okay, then I'll do some research over the next few weeks and see if I can drum up some freelance work. And remember I'm going to a wedding in Colorado over Labor Day weekend, so maybe I can find some work from my old contacts there. People do a lot of telecommuting these days."

Lying in bed in the dark that night, I thought about re-launching my business career. It seemed like a daunting task. Now I was more suited to being a chauffeur, a laundress or a medical assistant.

Questions flooded my sleepless mind. How could I incorporate my caregiver experience into a new job? Could I go back into the stringent corporate environment and if so, could I possibly find a company to work for that cared about its people as much as its profit? What did I want to do with the rest of my life? What did I feel passionate about?

During the night I dreamt I was in a beauty salon getting my hair highlighted and Vanna was with me. She was asleep on the floor next to my chair, but suddenly someone slipped and spilled some horrible toxic gel all over her. I jumped from the chair and grabbed her. The gel burned my skin and I was terrified about what it was doing to Vanna. I rushed outside the salon and looked for a hose. I could see one in the distance, but I had to cross a small grassy field that was literally covered with awful, smelly dog poop. I was so afraid that Vanna was dying that I just marched through the poop and finally got her to a place where I could turn the hose on her. When I hosed her down, she was fine and the poop had disappeared from our path. Vanna and I frolicked together across the field back to the beauty salon where a big celebration awaited us.

When I awoke, the dream was still vivid and I thought about its symbolism. Did Vanna represent my parents? Was the field of poop a corporate office? And what about that toxic gel? Was it my ego? Whatever it was, I decided then and there to re-focus on settling my parents and stop worrying about a new job until they were taken care of.

TWENTY-SEVEN
HOW DO YOU EAT AN ELEPHANT?

I know God will not give me anything I can't handle. I just wish he didn't trust me so much.
- Mother Teresa of Calcutta

The morning after my strange dream, I had to go to the hospital for a meeting with Jack's doctors, Mom's doctor, hospital social worker, representatives from the caregiver agency, plus Mom, Jack, Ted and Meg. It seemed as if we had a small army crowded into Jack's room. Several of us sat on his bed and others leaned against walls. Mom was sitting in the one chair in the room with a deer in the headlights look on her face. She had been bewildered ever since I had picked her up.

During the ride to the hospital, Mom said, "This is the end of my life, I just know it. I hate what is happening. I don't want strangers in my home, but I know we need them for Jack. I just don't know what to think," she said.

"Then don't think about it. Try to stay in the present moment and go with the flow," I said, knowing that she might not grasp such a concept.

"How can I go with the flow when it's all flowing at me?" she asked.

"I guess you just have to keep your heart and mind open to all that is flowing at you and know that you will be taken care of. Now is the time to trust in God," I said.

After a few seconds of silence, Mom said, "I

think I can do that."

"Remember Mom, Meg and John and I are not going to let anything bad happen to you or Jack," I said.

Jack's doctor spoke first. "We are here because I need to go over with all of you what Jack is going to need when we release him tomorrow," he said to the audience in the cramped room. Then he outlined the things we would need to do: Prepare the apartment for a disabled senior citizen, order oxygen, line up physical therapists and nurses to come to the apartment regularly and secure a round-the-clock caregiver service.

Mom's doctor noticed the fearful look on her face and chimed in, "We also have to think about Marianne's care. She is going to need some support, too. And long term, you all must consider an alternative to independent apartment living." All I could think was, ouch. But Mom took it pretty well. She trusted her doctor and didn't appear to be threatened.

After the meeting, I spent some time with the social worker who suggested we set up some in-home therapy for Mom so she would feel attention was being paid to her, too. I loved that idea. I had been taking her to outpatient physical therapy for months. This would be an easy transition.

The following day, Jack was released from the hospital at noon. Unfortunately, he went right back that night due to diabetic complications. His blood sugar was so high that we called the paramedics to come and check him out. It had been exactly one week since his last ambulance

ride and sure enough, Charlie, the driver Mom
liked was one of the paramedics who responded
to our call.

"Hello Charlie," Mom said.

"Hello Marianne," he replied. "Are you
ready to go for another ride?"

"No, I think I'll stay home tonight," she
said. She was already dressed in her nightgown
and bathrobe. I was proud of her for declining
Charlie's invitation because she was conscious
of her own exhaustion and knew she couldn't
accomplish anything positive by going to the
hospital.

"Meg and I can drive in my car," I told
Charlie. "Although Mom says you're an excellent
driver." His chuckle took a little of the edge off
the uneasiness of paramedics preparing Jack to
be transported back to the emergency room.

Jack's return to the hospital for three days
actually helped. A renovated apartment was
available and it was right next door to the one
they were currently occupying. Mom didn't like
the idea of moving, but she understood. The
whole situation was overwhelming for her and
I was worried that it might trigger one of her
depressions, but thankfully, she appeared to be
resilient.

Mom and Jack had moved from a big house
into the little apartment seven years earlier.
Although they had downsized dramatically, they
still had a lot of furniture and other belongings
in storage. And they had also accumulated a lot
of stuff in the last seven years.

"How are we going to do this with so little
time?" Meg asked me.

"How do you eat an elephant," I joked.

"Yeah, I know, one bite at a time. Ugh."

Meg and I went through all of the drawers, closets and cupboards and got rid of things we knew our parents wouldn't miss. We knew Gary and Ted could handle moving all the furniture, as it was just going around a corner to the apartment next door. I called the moving company that had helped Gary and me. They agreed to do the move in three days. I told Meg, "There, we have another bite of the elephant," and she cracked up.

Jack was released from the hospital again, and this time he seemed to be okay. Mom hated having the second-shift caregivers in her living room all night. We purchased a baby monitor so the caregiver could hear sounds to know when Jack had to get up to go to the bathroom. Mom told me endlessly every day that she could handle Jack alone at night; and I kept responding that she could not. This was the first time I felt I had become my mother's parent. It was very uncomfortable, but I remembered that Jacqueline Marcell had survived it, and I knew I could do the same.

Within a couple of weeks, things had settled down and my parents were getting into a new routine with their caregivers. They still expected me to come over at least once a day, mostly to listen to their comments and complaints, or hang out with them. I was determined to keep that routine for awhile because I knew that simply to disappear would be very hard on all of us. We had to wean ourselves from the daily companionship we had enjoyed over the past year.

By Labor Day weekend, I was calm and
knew I could go to the wedding in Colorado
without worrying. As I packed, I realized I felt
almost giddy about getting away. Gary had
decided to drive to Wyoming to attend a family
reunion with his sister and to pick up a 1964
Ford Mustang he had purchased to restore. We
both needed time out from all the stress, even
before we went on vacation.

TWENTY-EIGHT
I CAN SEE CLEARLY NOW

*If your knowledge of fire has been turned to
certainty by words alone, then seek to be cooked by
the fire itself. Don't abide in borrowed certainty. There
is no real certainty until you burn; if you wish for this,
sit down in the fire.*

- Rumi

The wedding in Colorado would provide the
opportunity to see old friends and co-workers.
This time, I looked forward to seeing everyone
without feeling the least bit inferior or resentful
about my new way of life.

A week before, I had completed an exercise
from William Bridges' book, *Transitions*. In the
book, Bridges asks the questions, "What are
the events that have brought change into your
life in the past year? And what are the areas
of your life in which the changes are evident?"
He asked that the reader write about his or her
experiences, in five categories:

1) Losses of Relationships
2) Changes in Home Life
3) Personal Changes
4) Work and Financial Changes
5) Inner Changes

I wrote each question in my journal and then
scribbled out the answers. My goal was to shed some
light on what I wanted to do with my life now that I
was not going to be a full-time caregiver.

There was no mistake that "Losses of Relationships" was first. Tears streamed down my cheeks as I wrote about the loss of closeness with my brother. He had so much going on in his life that he had virtually disappeared from mine. I had expected to come back to California and reclaim him as an instant best friend, but that didn't happen. I wrote a commitment to myself not to give up on John and to know that our relationship could be repaired someday.

"Changes in Home Life" had been gigantic. We had moved twice in one year. The long escrow for the purchase of our new home was a huge emotional burden at times. We were still remodeling and living in an unsettled environment.

Our home life now included an open door to Cory and Emilie. We were thrilled to have them close by and to share free time with them. The arrival of the baby in November was cause for great joy. But it was also very different from Colorado where we had no family and our personal time was always our own unless we chose to invite someone to our home.

Reflecting on "Personal Changes," I wrote about the dramatic shift in roles that Gary and I had undergone since our move. When we lived in Colorado, I used to go to work every weekday morning. I got a paycheck every Friday and had a pattern for paying our bills and setting aside money for savings. Gary worked from home. He collected money from his various jobs and hung out with the pets. He cleaned the house and garage. Every evening when I arrived home, we sat and talked about my day.

Now our roles were reversed. Gary left for work very early every morning, usually before 5 a.m. He collected the weekly paycheck. I worked with and for my parents, hung out with our pets in the mornings and did an occasional freelance writing project. At night, we talked about his day.

By far the best change in my personal relationships had evolved from rekindled California friendships and membership in The Inside Edge. My old friends—Dru, Kathy, Marianne, Terry and Vicki—were an invaluable part of my new life, and I had many new friends from The Edge who seemed like old friends after only a few months of getting to know them.

"Work and Financial Changes" were huge too. My income had decreased dramatically and of course, my job had changed. Worse, I had spent a lot of my savings trying to keep up a semblance of the lifestyle I had enjoyed while I was working. While journaling about this area, I realized that I had to do something that would bring in more money. I would have to do it soon.

The "Inner Changes" were more complicated to write about. Thanks to The Edge and our church, The Center for Universal Truth, my spiritual connections had been re-established. This helped me feel more peaceful and positive about all the changes occurring in my life.

The peaceful, positive feelings were juxtaposed against my scary, negative feelings about going back to work. I wrote about wanting to work at home and perhaps write a book, but I didn't feel qualified to write anything meaningful because I did not have an advanced degree. My previously published work amounted to a few magazine articles. I had to confront these inner fears before I could make any progress toward my next career steps.

The exercise of writing about transitions helped me chart a new career path. When it was over, I knew I wanted to keep my freedom and work from home. I also knew I had to research and then canvas some of my mentors and friends about the kind of work I wanted to do. Most important of all, I had a burning desire to write for a living.

Writing had been my passion since I was 14 years old; I liked to talk to people, too. I had enjoyed public speaking and wanted to do more of it, given the opportunity. With or without an advanced degree, I knew in my heart I had something important to say and needed to get it out there.

While packing that night, I noticed my dog-eared copy of Dr. Wayne Dyer's *The Power of Intention*, in the pile of books that sat next to my bed. I picked it up and decided to take it with me on the plane. I wanted to re-read some of the chapters that I knew would help me take the next step in creating a new career working from home. Looking at the cover, I saw the subtitle, as if for the first time: *Learning to Co-create Your World Your Way*. Wow, I thought. *What a perfect opportunity for me right now.*

Over the long weekend with many of my dear friends, I felt more powerful than I had felt since I had departed Colorado 18 months ago. The wedding in Breckenridge was delightful. The mountain resort and the weather gods presented the newlyweds with an early snowstorm as a wedding gift.

Earlier in the day, everything had been set up outdoors when it was sunny and warm. Then the clouds covered the mountain and the snow began to fall just before the late afternoon ceremony. Many of us guests helped bring the flowers, the gorgeous white runner and some of the chairs indoors.

Nobody panicked, the bride was radiant, the groom was all smiles, and the bride's mom—my dear friend and former co-worker, Linda—was a calm and beautiful queen mother. The ceremony was warm and wonderful and the minister acknowledged everyone for trusting that all was good. Linda thanked me for spearheading the team that brought the runner indoors and I simply took a deep breath and said, "You are so welcome. I love you."

Later, in my Breckenridge hotel room, I read a line that I had highlighted in *The Power of Intention* and shivered at its synchronous application to my experience that day: "This new way of seeing will enable people in your presence to feel comforted and peaceful, and to indirectly be loving accomplices to your connection to intention." All I could think when I turned out the light was *Thank you, God.*

TWENTY-NINE
CRUISE CONTROL

*Twenty years from now you will be more
disappointed by the things you didn't do than by the
ones you did do. So throw off the bowlines. Sail away
from the safe harbor. Catch the trade winds in your
sails. Explore. Dream. Discover.*
                    - Mark Twain

No sooner had I returned from Colorado and
Gary from Wyoming than we were packing for our
cruise. New boundaries had been established
with Mom and Jack primarily because both
Gary and I had been out of town for five days.
They had been forced to rely on caregivers plus
Meg and Ted.

A few days before we were to leave, Jack had
to be hospitalized again. I spent twelve hours with
him in the emergency room because this time we
had decided not to call the paramedics. The ER
doctors diagnosed complications of congestive
heart failure. Although his condition was not
too serious, he would remain hospitalized for a
few days for observation. Mom and Meg insisted
that I go ahead with the cruise.

Cory and Emilie drove us to San Diego
where we boarded the Legend of the Seas, our
seagoing home for the next week. I felt elated
and profoundly grateful to spend a luxurious
week cruising with Gary.

Sailing out of San Diego harbor this sunny
September afternoon, I could not stop joyful
tears. Six months ago, I never would have

dreamed we'd be on a cruise to Mexico, or that we would be living in a cute little home of our own in Costa Mesa. Somehow, I knew this cruise would mark the end of an important transition in my life that had been filled with difficult lessons, exciting discoveries and important distinctions. I was feeling blissful, peaceful and connected. I wanted these feelings to continue and knew I had the power to make that happen.

On our first day at sea, I went to the spa and Gary went to the casino. We hung out by the pool for awhile, and then participated in a bingo game, which was cause for hearty laughter. We had only played bingo at sea. It reminded us that unbridled silliness often happens on vacations, and we loved the experience.

The next few days were relaxing and fun. We visited Cabo San Lucas, Mazatlan and Puerto Vallarta, marveling at the good weather. I was a bit concerned about Jack and whether or not he was out of the hospital yet, but Gary reminded me that Meg would contact us if there was a problem. I agreed to focus on the present and enjoy our vacation.

On our last night, Gary and I visited the Viking Crown Lounge. We went there every night after dinner so Gary could enjoy a fancy cigar and I could have a martini. Just as we were about to leave, the DJ played a song called *You are the Love of my Life*, by Sammy Kershaw. We both stopped in our tracks before reaching the elevator. This seldom-heard song had been played for our first dance at our wedding in 1999. The synchronicity of it all overwhelmed me as Gary took my hand and led me to the dance floor. We hadn't danced for several years and yet here we were dancing to "our song" on a cruise ship. Once again, I felt blissful and peaceful.

When we docked in San Diego the next morning, I simply didn't want to get out of bed. Gary had to drag me to the final breakfast on the ship. Waiting to disembark after breakfast, I felt kind of sick to my stomach – and I had never been seasick in my life.

The cruise had been an escape I didn't want to end. I recalled the feelings of power and peace I experienced when we left a week ago and suddenly realized I simply had to re-create them to turn my entire life into a blissful and peaceful experience. As Dr. Wayne Dyer says, "Change the way you look at things and the things you look at change." I knew in my heart that I could go from a dream vacation to a dream life, and the only thing that could get in the way of the unfolding of that dream life was me. I could put my life on "cruise control."

The following day, after unpacking, opening mail and doing the laundry, I went to my desk, turned on my computer and said to myself, "Welcome to your new career, Shannon." I made a few phone calls and by the end of the day, I had four clients and three more potential clients. I also called Reverend Sandy at the church office and offered to help with the newsletter as a volunteer editor.

Early the next morning, I started writing this book. My goal was to explore my journey from corporate executive to caregiver. I wanted to share the lessons of that journey with others who felt trapped and hopeless in their jobs or careers and wanted to find a way to a better, more fulfilling lifestyle.

PART TWO
FROM CORPORATE TO CARE

THIRTY
Eight Footprints on the Journey to Care

Be aware of wonder. Live a balanced life – learn some and think some and draw and paint and sing and dance and play and work every day some.
- Robert Fulghum

When I began writing this book, I asked many of my friends, associates and acquaintances if they thought it might have been possible for me to have figured out a way to care for my elderly parents while nourishing them, me and a full-time corporate career. Most people said, "That would depend on the corporation." In other words, it would be hard to carve out a balanced personal and professional life working for a company that was mean-spirited or morally and ethically bankrupt. I hoped it might be more about the individual than the company.

What I had received from my journey from corporate to care was the gift of approval: pats on the back from family and friends who

acknowledged my "doing the right thing." On
this path, I learned the sublime reward of
peace of mind, of knowing my behavior, choices
and actions were in line with goodness. The
journey had been profoundly exasperating and
humbling at times, but ultimately it was more
powerful than I had ever dreamed it could be
when I began.

Some of the men and women I spoke with
recalled leaving corporate careers to take care of
their young children. In part, the career change
was a way to sidestep the stress associated with
the corporate domain. A few people went back
to work for awhile when the kids started grade
school; but most chose to work as independent
consultants or find jobs in the non-profit realm,
real estate or retail. Their new careers were still
stressful, but allowed a more flexible schedule
than those in the traditional corporate sector.
People who made the leap felt better about
balancing work and family life. Their new jobs
gave them freedom to choose to attend a child's
softball game or spend a weekday afternoon with
an aging parent without the pressure of being at
a computer in a corporate cubicle.

John Graham, professor of International
Marketing at the University of California, Irvine,
told me there are two problems in American
management today which make it difficult for
corporations to be environments wherein people
respect and care for one another. The first is
the persistent notion that greed is good. This
came from Adam Smith, the founder of modern
economics, but it was made famous in the
1980s by financier Gordon Gecko, a notorious

character played by Michael Douglas in Oliver Stone's movie, *Wall Street*. The second problem is the general rule that in an economic downturn, companies must lay people off.

Adam Smith wrote the landmark book, *The Wealth of Nations*, in the 18th century. In one of its famous passages, he said, "It is not from the benevolence of the butcher, the brewer, or the baker, that we expect our dinner, but from their regard to their own interest. We address ourselves, not to their humanity but to their self-love, and never talk to them of our own necessities but of their advantage."[1]

These words from the father of modern economics led many people to believe Smith advocated greed and self-promotion. Ironically, what I learned during my religious science studies is Smith did not. He lived during the Enlightenment and wanted to counter the Church's view that any kind of self-interest was sinful. What he really thought about business was that people in general had an innate sense of what was morally virtuous. People want to do the right thing. They are disciplined by conscience. They want approval, but they also want to believe they deserve approval.

I have been blessed to work for a couple of successful companies with the magic touch of creativity, discipline, productivity and profit. These were companies where the dream was bigger than the individuals who held it. The atmosphere in these environments was dynamic and charged with positive energy even on the most difficult of days. Nobody called anyone Pollyanna; we were profitable and everyone felt

[1] *The Wealth of Nations*, Oxford University Press, 1976 [1776], pp. 26-27.

like a valuable contributor. In short, we cared deeply about our company.

I have also worked for companies where the atmosphere was tense and full of fear. Turnover was high and cynicism ruled the workforce. Invariably, the stink of trepidation emanated from the grinches in the highest executive suites and people were incessantly running for emotional cover, hiding in their cubicles and trying to plot a way to get out. These were also places where a dramatic "we" and "they" segmentation existed between the executive class and "everyone else." The senior executives rarely asked middle management or people on the front lines for input. Instead they hired expensive professional consulting firms with hordes of MBAs who came in, created processes, added technology and laid people off.

The journey from corporate to care taught me much more than how to care for my elderly parents. I had excellent resources to support me in making sure their care was in place. Some of those resources are listed in the Appendix. More importantly, I learned about the qualities that I now refer to as the eight footprints on my journey to care. By the end of the journey, I had developed the ability to care for myself and so to care for others.

You do not have to be a Ph.D. psychologist, Oprah or a Buddhist monk to discover your own peace of mind this lifetime. You simply need to have the desire for balance. And you must know what is in your personal "pot of gold" at the end of your own rainbow. As Dr. Phil McGraw says, "You have to name it to claim it."[2]

[2] *Life Strategies-Doing What Works, Doing What Matters*, Phillip C. McGraw, Ph.D., Hyperion, 1999, p. 211

Before I left my corporate job, I wrote in my journal what I wanted to create in my life and what I would have to change in order to get it. Through journaling I learned that my parents were still very important to me and I wanted to give something back to them. I wanted to give my siblings with small children the space to care for their nuclear families. I could only do that by putting my career on hold and moving back home. For me, moving to California from Colorado seemed like a daunting step — leaving my job, moving to my old hometown and asking my husband to come with me. Yet once committed to claiming this new life, I discovered I had the courage to make it happen.

The same exercise of chronicling my life's "wish list" helped me to change my role from full-time family caregiver to writer. When I discovered I could no longer handle care for my parents without additional professional assistance, I had the opportunity to change careers again, but wanted to stay close to Mom and Jack to be available if they needed me. Clearly, I did not want to go back to an environment that didn't support my caregiver track, so I chose to work for myself out of my home office.

So what are the eight footprints on the journey to care and how do you make them work for you? In the following chapters, I explain the eight footprints. You can use them to step into your full potential to care for yourself and others in ways you may not have understood in the past, and you do not have to leave your job in the corporate world to do it.

THIRTY-ONE
THE FIRST FOOTPRINT: SELF-ESTEEM

There is overwhelming evidence that the higher the level of self-esteem, the more likely one will be to treat others with respect, kindness and generosity.
- Nathaniel Branden

The first footprint is self-esteem. There have been many books written about self-esteem, but my favorite is probably the most basic, a little book titled, *How to Raise Your Self-Esteem*, by the renowned authority on the subject, Dr. Nathaniel Branden. Dr. Branden defines self-esteem as the sum of self-confidence and self-respect.

Dr. Branden is one of my heroes. In the late 1980s when I was going through some personal crises including a new job working for Disneyland that I didn't feel competent to accept, a friend recommended *How to Raise your Self-Esteem* to me. I read it on a plane. By the time I finished it and completed most of the exercises that he recommended, I felt downright empowered to take that new job. I hadn't changed, but how I perceived myself had changed, thanks to insights I had gained.

About six months after reading the book, I recommended it to someone on my staff at Disneyland. That same day, I wrote a letter to Dr. Branden and thanked him for his pioneering work in self-esteem development. About a week later, I was shocked when my assistant buzzed my phone and said, "I have a call for you from

Nathaniel Branden on line one." I thought it was one of my friends playing a trick on me, but answered in my normal business tone of voice and sure enough, it really was Dr. Branden. He thanked me for my letter and asked if I would be interested in talking with him about some work that he was doing on the importance of self-esteem in the workplace. I was in shock, but said yes and a week later he joined me for lunch at the Disneyland Hotel.

I doubt anything could have boosted my self-esteem the way having lunch with Nathaniel Branden did. I sat in the restaurant trying not to stare in awe at this wise, articulate man who had taken the time to come and meet with me. I shared some of my experiences of the way one's self-esteem can be shattered by a psychopathic boss, or by comparing oneself to a co-worker in a way that brings up feelings of inadequacy. Any of those situations can start a person with average self-esteem on a downward spiral at work. Dr. Branden commented about how the same thing happens to young children in school, but it is not a totally passive process. We have a choice in how we respond.

Dr. Branden was a kind of Fairy Godfather to my Cinderella that day at Disneyland. I was just your average middle manager in a huge corporation, but suddenly I knew I was special. I realized I could make a positive difference for myself and others if I maintained a healthy sense of self-esteem.

That almost spiritual realization led to believing that supporting people's high self-esteem is crucial to honing their ability to attain balance between work and home life. Over the next few years after I met Dr. Branden, I coached all my team members to face their demons and fears and climb the self-esteem ladder. I've heard that "we teach what we most need to learn," and this was true for me while taking on the self-esteem challenge at work. In coaching my staff, I learned how to keep my own self-esteem up in the face of all kinds of change, criticism and rejection.

How can we ever hope to care for someone or something important to us if we can't care for ourselves? When I was a nerdy high school teenager, I had very low self-esteem. My loser mentality was grounded in a belief that I was overweight and looked bad in a bikini. I chose to hang out with other losers because we had so much in common. We even called ourselves the "Rejects and Losers Club." I wore my nerdiness like a badge of honor, and then suddenly everything changed at the end of my senior year. Our family doctor put me on a low calorie diet and told me to take a 30 minute walk every day. I lost 20 pounds. Mom bought me some new clothes. I went to a dance in another town with my "Rejects and Losers Club" friends and lots of attractive boys asked me to dance. I felt pretty and intelligent, but humbled because I was still the same person, only thinner. I didn't want to be a nerd any more, but wanted to keep my old friends—and am still close to many of them today. All of us were late-bloomers.

The lesson I learned from losing that 20 pounds in high school was that I'm responsible for how I feel and—most important—I am the only one who can change me. Taking responsibility and changing how I looked and felt by getting into better physical condition raised my self-esteem. With higher self-esteem, I telegraphed both confidence and humility to the people I met. Nowadays, even in the midst of menopause, whenever I slack off from my exercise regimen, good eating habits and emotional health, I get right back on as soon as I can in order to avoid a drop in self-esteem. Without high self-esteem we tend to focus on what is wrong with our lives rather than what is good and lose focus of what we care about, including ourselves.

THIRTY-TWO
THE SECOND FOOTPRINT: COURAGE

Courage is going from failure to failure without losing enthusiasm.
> *- Winston Churchill*

My friend, David Neenan, is a businessman and commercial real estate developer in Colorado—whose hobby is teaching a seminar called *Business & You*. He offers a variety of tools to students to help them take responsibility for their lives, personally and professionally. A key tool featured in David's workshop is courage and I always liked his definition of the word which was inspired by psychologist Rollo May who wrote *The Courage to Create*:

Courage = Commitment + Doubt

Recently, I read another definition of courage: "Courage is acting despite your fears." So I have changed David's definition to:

Courage = Commitment + Doubt + Action

The most familiar incidents of courage are the ones we see in the news every day—heroic split decisions where someone rushes into a burning building or jumps into an icy river to save a child. Slightly less publicized but equally impressive are the long term acts of courage in the face of a serious illness like cancer or a debilitating car accident.

Common courage is what most of us
summon daily. It's the courage to walk out of a
meeting with an abusive boss, to be happy while
confronting a failed relationship, to face the
numbers on the scale on the day after vacation
ends, to make that series of cold calls, to take the
car keys away from your father who shouldn't
be driving, to stand up and speak to a crowd
of strangers. Common courage is an important
footprint on the journey to care because the
journey often requires taking action in spite of
our fears, being committed to an outcome while
doubting we can achieve it.

Courage usually means taking the hard way
rather than the easy way. A friend of mine once
told me that in many situations, if one choice is
harder than another, the harder one is probably
the correct one, and it takes courage to make
that difficult choice.

Caring for yourself takes courage. When
you care about yourself, you stand up for
your ideas and principles. You are ethical and
compassionate. You know that, in the words of
Buckminster Fuller, "Integrity is the essence of
everything successful." You confront your inner
demons, real or imagined. You summon the
courage to forgo fast foods for healthy ones, and
exercise often so that your body stays in shape.

I knew I would not have peace of mind for the
rest of my life if I didn't go back to my hometown
and take care of my parents. As a middle-aged
woman, I was terrified of leaving a good, stable
job in the corporate world even for the short-
term. My husband was willing to come with me,
but we had no idea what he would do for a living

in a new state. I listened to my heart and simply knew I had to take action. It took great courage to do what we did and now we acknowledge ourselves for it. Yet we are constantly faced with new decisions and challenges on our journey that require even more common courage.

THIRTY-THREE
THE THIRD FOOTPRINT: AWARENESS

*The aim of life is to live, and to live means to be
aware, joyously, drunkenly, serenely, divinely aware.*
- Henry Miller

How can you care if you are not aware?
Let's say you care deeply about the welfare and
safety of children. You contribute money to
UNICEF and your local children's hospital. Then,
while driving to work one day you reach for your
cell phone, look down for a couple of seconds
to dial a number and — BOOM — something
bounces off the right front fender of your car.
Suddenly you are screaming, smashing your
foot onto the brake pedal and looking into the
rear view mirror to see a small body lying at the
side of the road behind you. Your heart is in
your throat and you are sick to your stomach.
And you are aware. If only you had been aware
30 seconds earlier.

This happened to me. It was a lovely day in
1985 and the distraction wasn't a cell phone. It
was my penchant for daydreaming while driving
alone and a gorgeous view of the ocean glittering
in the afternoon sun while I was descending
from the hills of Pacific Heights in Honolulu.
Lost in my reverie, I didn't notice a small city
bus stopped on the left side of the road, nor did I
see the small boy run from behind the bus until
just before I hit him. I swerved madly to the
right but he still bounced off my car and onto
the pavement. My car stopped on someone's

front lawn and screaming, I ran from the car to the boy, who looked to be about three years old and was crying loudly. He had abrasions on his arms and legs and was bleeding slightly from a head wound. His mother had run from the bus and thrown herself on the ground next to him, wailing.

Several other passengers and the bus driver rushed into the street, which thankfully was not a busy one. The bus driver called 911 and told us to leave the little boy where he was and that it was a good sign he was crying. He asked if anyone spoke Chinese because he knew the boy's mother spoke no English. An older woman passenger said yes, and she communicated with the distraught mother in Mandarin, telling her that the police and paramedics were on the way. All I could say was, "I am so sorry. I am so sorry."

Today, I remember all of this as if it were a terrible nightmare. The witnesses reported to the police that the boy had run out from behind the bus just as I was driving past, and that I was not exceeding the speed limit. I told the police I simply did not see him, but admitted that I had been a bit distracted by the view of the ocean. The car was towed to a repair shop and my husband, Bruce, came to pick me up. We went to the hospital emergency room to find out about the boy and discovered that he had a minor concussion and would be released later in the day. His father was there and he spoke English. He thanked us for our concern.

When the initial shock of the accident wore off later that night, and I was sure the child would be fine, I began to see the entire experience as a metaphor. I had been driving the company car that day. It was the first time I had asked to use the car in the six years I had worked there. For several months, I had felt trapped and unhappy in my job and had wanted to leave. I wanted to start my own company, but felt that I couldn't afford to give up my salary and benefits. Lying in bed that night thinking about what had happened during this painful and frightening experience, I became aware that I had to quit my job.

I saw myself as the little boy, excited about life and wanting to create and be free to make different kinds of decisions than the company's policies demanded, and then running head-on into the automobile, which represented management — a wall that I had been bumping into constantly for a year. If I couldn't summon the courage to get out of the company or resign myself to bowing to management's demands, then I risked a more serious health consequence in the months to come. This awareness opened up an empowering new state of consciousness in which I saw myself flying over the wall.

Two days after the accident, I submitted my letter of resignation. Two months later, I had my own company. And many years later, I am pricked by the memory of that little boy whenever I reach for my makeup or am tempted to look down at my cell phone while driving, and by the memory of quitting my job whenever I feel stuck in a situation that requires action over daydreaming.

My dear friend, Carol Edmonston, author of

Connections: The Sacred Journey Between Two Points, gave me this great three-step process to stay aware:

Step 1) Breathe in.

Step 2) Breathe out.

Step 3) Repeat steps one and two.

It's amazing how the simple act of noticing how you breathe in and out helps to expand your awareness. You can take it a step further with this next awareness exercise.

Sit in a comfortable chair with your arms and legs uncrossed, feet firmly on the ground in front of you, shoulders relaxed, eyes closed. Take a deep breath and as you breathe in, feel the air as it fills your lungs, then gently let it go. Wiggle your toes and fingers, and then breathe in and out again. Now place your awareness just above and behind your head and notice your body in the chair. As you slowly and deeply breathe in and out, notice your sensations and feelings as they move in and out of your awareness. Notice any thoughts, images and sounds in this natural and relaxed state of awareness as you breathe.

This simple exercise is a painless way to expand your awareness and inner clarity. Remember, to feel pain is to be aware. To feel sadness is to be aware. To feel joy is to be aware. To feel nothing is to be numb. Awareness is an invaluable tool to help you connect to that which you must do to care for yourself and others.

THIRTY-FOUR
THE FOURTH FOOTPRINT: FORGIVENESS

*We achieve inner health only through forgiveness
— the forgiveness not only of others but also of
ourselves.*

- Joshua Loth Liebman

Forgiveness is a tool of completion. It allows us to move on. When we choose to forgive someone or something that has hurt or injured us, then we have chosen to cross a spiritual bridge to peace instead of blowing up the bridge with resentment, internal struggle and strife. Forgiveness lets us shake off the bonds of self-imposed victimization and resignation. Forgiveness is the footprint of freedom.

My father chose to leave our family when I was still a child. He rented an apartment not far from our home where my brother and I could visit him on weekends. It wasn't the same as having him around every night, helping with homework and making the music that made our home feel like a magical place. He left us with our bipolar mom who loved us more than life itself, but whose unpredictable mood swings sometimes made it hard to maintain a peaceful home. When Mom was in a sad or angry mood, Dad always diverted us with music and silly stories. Dad made us believe that the mere act of smiling could change the world. Dad was right.

He came back for about a year and then he left forever. And this time when he left, he didn't leave a forwarding address. The pain of his alcoholic life was too great for him to stay or be anywhere close to his children. John and I were in our early teens and didn't understand his pain; we only understood that he had abandoned us, something our mom reinforced constantly. At a time when our friends were groovin' to The Beach Boys, The Beatles and The Doors, we had lost our music, our smiles and our desire to do anything but watch television. We spent endless hours watching monotonous TV, from *The Mod Squad* to *The Monkees* to *Marcus Welby, M.D.* John left the TV to play basketball a few afternoons a week, but I stayed and numbed out watching shows like *Dark Shadows* and *Another World*— even *Sesame Street,* just to escape the pain.

In 1987, 20 years after my dad moved out of my life, I found him living in a trailer park in Ft. Collins, Colorado. I had tracked him down through his second wife's daughter. I had an address and phone number and knew if I dialed that number, I would hear his voice.

All I wanted to do was tell Dad how much he had hurt me by disappearing when I was a teenager. I wanted to ask him if he had any lingering pangs of guilt about what he had done to John and me. I wanted to scream and yell and pound my fists and tell him how he had practically ruined our lives. And I wanted to let him know that we had found a great new dad in our stepfather, Jack. But when I finally dialed the number and he answered, I simply gasped and said, "Hi Daddy, this is Shannie," followed by uncontrollable sobs. Years of pain and bitterness and unrequited love spilled out with my tears. All he said, over and over, was, "It's okay sweetie. I understand. I'm glad you called. I understand."

I remember feeling as if a dam of forgiveness had broken and washed away all the hurt and anger and resignation. My dad didn't have to tell me what made him do what he did. I understood. And I forgave him. That unspoken forgiveness allowed me to listen to him talk about his life since he left John and me. I listened as he talked about his pain and hopelessness, his long battle with alcoholism and recovery, and about his belief that he could only cause us harm if he tried to reconnect. He talked about how much he had loved my mom. And finally, he asked me if I could ever forgive him for abandoning us. I said yes, and in that moment I felt complete for the first time in decades.

Forgiveness allows us to face what we have created in the past, acknowledge our mistakes, and move on. Its benefits come not only from the act of forgiving, but also from asking for forgiveness and being forgiven. Sometimes, even when we humbly and sincerely ask for forgiveness, it will not be granted. Then our challenge is to accept the consequences, forgive ourselves, and move on, knowing that we have rewritten our memory of a past bad event and taken an important step on our own path to care.

THIRTY-FIVE
THE FIFTH FOOTPRINT: FAITH

What lies behind us and what lies before us are tiny matters compared to what lies within us.
- Ralph Waldo Emerson

When I was a child attending catechism classes on Monday afternoons at a little church on Balboa Island, I had trouble conceptualizing God as someone who would send a little baby to hell if it hadn't been baptized before it died. Friends of my parents lost a baby at childbirth and one of the kids in my class kept insisting that the baby went straight to hell. My mom told me to ignore the remark and that God had room for all babies up in heaven. I had a lot more faith in my mom than in God at that point, yet somehow I believed that God had passed that message on to Mom to give to me.

I have always been blessed with faith. I never labeled my faith as "religion," although I have always had profound respect for religions of the world. Ethical principles are at the heart of every religion, so with that in mind, I have always believed in "a higher power." One of my college boyfriends told me he was an agnostic who believed in The Big Bang theory of creation. I asked him: "What do you think created The Big Bang?" We didn't date much after that.

I left the Catholic Church shortly after my parents divorced, but still believed in God. Over the years, I joined friends at different churches and in a wide variety of spiritual pursuits until I finally settled on a simple faith that allows me to honor God and respect all religions. This faith has served as a strong foundation to guide me through difficult times, from Bruce's death to confrontations with tyrant bosses to supporting friends who are seriously ill to caring for my elderly parents.

In her book, *Positive Energy*, Dr. Judith Orloff says, "No one can dictate your spiritual identity for you. If you were turned off or made cynical by early religious upbringing, start fresh. Try not to get mixed up by other people's opinions." She offers helpful guidelines[3] for discovering your own sense of spirit and says that hundreds of scientific studies have shown that spirituality catalyzes energy.

Another one of my modern day heroes is the author and life coach, Iyanla Vanzant. I had the pleasure of listening to Iyanla several years ago when she visited Mile Hi Church in Denver. In her book, *Faith in the Valley: Lessons for Women on the Journey to Peace*, Iyanla reminds us that we are never really alone because God is always by our side. More importantly, you are always by your side. No matter how dire and bleak the situation might seem for you when you are experiencing one of life's valleys, you just need a little faith in yourself to get through it, and maybe some guidance to find that faith in yourself.

My faith is constantly catalyzed by signs. Corny as it might sound, whenever I see a double rainbow, I know something wonderful is about to happen. If my feet tingle when I am meditating, I am reminded that God is pushing me upward.

[3] *Positive Energy*, Judith Orloff, M.D., Harmony Books, 2004, p. 60

When I am feeling down or scared, I say, "Show me the way," and invariably something happens very quickly to guide me back into a higher energy field. When that occurs, my faith is strengthened, yet I know that simply having faith is a treasure in and of itself.

THIRTY-SIX
THE SIXTH FOOTPRINT: HUMOR

If you can't make it better, you can laugh at it.
- Erma Bombeck

One of my favorite quotes from the *Bible* is "A merry heart doeth good like medicine" (Proverbs 17:22). I have discovered it is true. Laughing with my friends, at the antics of my pets, or even at myself, has proven to be my best antidote for stress.

Someone once told me that the mere act of smiling makes you feel better. Try it right now. Take a deep breath. Now smile, sincerely. How do you feel?

Norman Cousins, author of *Anatomy of an Illness*, the superb book on humor therapy, said, "Laughter is a powerful way to tap positive emotions." And comedian Bill Cosby says, "You can turn painful situations around through laughter. If you can find humor in anything, even poverty, you can survive it."

My journey from corporate to care has been filled with humor and laughter. In the worst of times, I found solace through laughing at myself or my response to something that was happening. When I could find and then share the humor in a painful situation with friends, it was easier to move through it.

I do not advocate humor as a way to bypass or suppress the experience of feeling pain, sadness, and grief. But laughter is a wonderful coping tool in our toolbox for dealing with suffering. It is a great way to release tension in our bodies and diffuse anxiety. Since the publication of Cousins' book in 1964, interest in the effects of humor on patients with serious diseases has grown to the point of spawning a new medical field—psycho-neuro immunology (PIN) which studies how the brain and the immune system interact. Researchers have discovered that laughter has all kinds of positive effects on the body, from lowering blood pressure to boosting the immune function. Laughter triggers the release of endorphins, the body's natural painkillers, producing a sense of peace and well-being.

Life does not cease to be serious when we laugh. We do not go instantly from tragedy and grief to joy. We experience a healing process that involves a wide range of emotions including joy, if we are lucky.

When Bruce died, I was consumed with sadness and grief. For weeks after his funeral, I would cry in my car where no one could hear me. Or so I thought. One day while driving down the mountain from my home in Conifer, Colorado, to my office in Englewood, I was having my morning cry, this time screaming from the pit of my stomach. Suddenly a huge splash of bird poop landed on my windshield, probably from a magpie. The splatter was at least 12 inches in diameter. Blinded by tears and bird doo, I pulled over to the side of the road. As I grabbed a paper towel and my scraper from the back of my Jeep, I started laughing hysterically and had to lean against the car. The bird's timing could not have been any better. It made me think that

Bruce was trying to tell me to brighten up and I felt great for the rest of that day recounting the story to my friends at work.

Dacher Keltner, a professor of psychology at the University of California, Berkeley, conducted a study that showed that people who laugh in the months following the death of a spouse are in better emotional shape and function better years later than people who express more negative emotions during their grief. His findings indicated that when people laugh while talking about distressing things, they move away from the negative emotions of the experience.[4] Anger and bitterness are very real feelings during mourning, and suppressing emotion is not the answer. Keltner observed that people who laughed during grief also expressed negative emotions.

I remember that whenever a big black cloud of economic issues, shareholder dissatisfaction, turnover and poor morale shrouded the company I worked for, joy and humor were hard to come by. People who feel stressed at work find it hard to express or experience joy on the job. Often, those are the times when laughter is the only way to help employees get their energy and enthusiasm back up where it belongs. Is it any wonder that Internet jokes and funny stories circulate more frequently during the toughest times at work?

People are drawn to people who make them laugh or who can laugh with them. Humor is an instant way to harness positive thoughts and release negative feelings. As such, it is an important element in taking care of yourself and others.

[4] *Smile, Though Your Heart Is Breaking* by Patricia McBroom, University of California at Berkeley News, 1997.

THIRTY-SEVEN
THE SEVENTH FOOTPRINT: ACTION

Don't wait. The time will never be just right.
- Napoleon Hill

Nothing happens without action. If you're sitting on your butt thinking about something you want to do, then you are not doing it. We are foiled by thoughts that what we want to accomplish, from cleaning out the garage to writing a book to getting a new job is such a gigantic undertaking that we don't know where to start. So we don't start. The truth is everything we want to do can be broken down into small steps. Chinese Taoist Philosopher Lao Tzu said, "A journey of a thousand miles must begin with the first step."

I am a recovering procrastinator. Until a few years ago, my motto was, "Always put off until tomorrow what you don't want to do today." It was something I learned in high school. I kept delaying to the very last minute things like writing term papers, studying for essay tests and constructing science projects. I still got by with a B average and that felt like a reward for procrastinating.

My high school habit of dodging things I didn't want to do continued into my adult life as paying bills a little late, leaving breakfast dishes in the sink and vacuuming only when company was coming. It was easier to sit in my office working on the computer until it was too late to go to the health club for a cardio work-out. I would say to myself, "Oh well, I guess I just have to go home and fix dinner."

It took about 10 business seminars to snap me out of my debilitating procrastination mode. I remember having a big "aha moment" in a seminar called "Choices" about facing my fears and taking small steps to do some things I wanted to do, like increasing my income and spending more quality time with my husband. I could see procrastination was a choice, and by making that choice I was sabotaging myself. I began to do little things that could contribute to achieving my goals. I posted W.H. Murray's excerpt about "Commitment" from *The Scottish Himalaya Expedition*, 1951 (see below) on my refrigerator. Paying my bills on time and cleaning the bedroom closet became important demonstrations of my newfound commitment to action. Procrastination became the enemy of my personal integrity.

....

Until one is committed, there is hesitancy, the chance to draw back, always ineffectiveness. Concerning all acts of initiative (and creation), there is one elementary truth the ignorance of which kills countless ideas and splendid plans: that the moment one definitely commits oneself, then providence moves too. A whole stream of events issues from the decision, raising in one's favor all manner of unforeseen incidents, meetings and material assistance, which no man could have dreamt would have come his way. I learned a deep respect for one of Goethe's couplets:

**Whatever you can do or dream you can, begin it.
Boldness has genius, power and magic in it!**

When I started feeling good about doing today what I could easily have put off till tomorrow, I knew I had broken the procrastination habit. It still rears its ugly head from time to time, mostly when I am overwhelmed with tasks and deadlines. That's when I write everything down and decide the order in which I will begin to do each one.

Psychologist Robert Maurer is director of behavioral sciences for the Family Practice Residency Program at Santa Monica UCLA Medical Center and a faculty member of the UCLA School of Medicine. He has written a wonderful book called *One Small Step Can Change Your Life – Using the Japanese Technique of Kaizen to Achieve Lasting Success.* Kaizen is the art of making great and lasting change through small steps and it has been used successfully by several *Fortune* 500 companies to outperform their competitors. Dr. Maurer has taken kaizen a step further and shown us how to integrate its wisdom into our personal lives. When I heard him speak at a meeting of The Inside Edge, he said his research was proving that people who succeed in their careers, personal relationships and health are people who take action in small, trivial steps to accomplish large goals.

Oprah Winfrey said, "My philosophy is that not only are you responsible for your life, but doing the best at this moment puts you in the best place for the next moment." I would add that doing your best to care for yourself at this moment puts you in a great place to care for your family or friends when they need you. Do it now.

THIRTY-EIGHT
THE EIGHTH FOOTPRINT: LOVE

You never lose by loving. You always lose by holding back.

- Barbara de Angelis

Love is what propelled me on my journey from corporate to care. I had to trust in my love for my parents, the love my husband, Gary, felt for me, the love of my career and most of all, unconditional love for myself.

In 1985, I was invited to work on the 12th International Human Unity Conference in Hawaii. My role was to handle public relations and coordinate interviews for the conference organizers, featured speakers and the local press. Little did I know that my "work" would facilitate some of the most profound conversations of my life.

Dr. Gerald Jampolsky, author of *Love is Letting Go of Fear*, and his wife, Diane Cirincione, were participants in one such conversation. I had recently read Dr. Jampolsky's book – twice. It's a little book with a huge message about eliminating the fear that stands in the way of our experience of love. Jampolsky believes that fear is created by our preoccupation with the past and the future. By staying in the present, we can let go of fear and experience peace of mind. This little book supported me in letting my first husband, Bruce, go live and work in California while I stayed in Hawaii. It gave me tools to stop worrying and just focus on the love that I felt for him and for our relationship.

I will never forget the open, kind and enthusiastic way that Jerry and Diane made my acquaintance that day on the windward side of Oahu. Jerry walked into the press room, extended his hand and said with a big smile, "Hi Shannon, I'm Jerry Jampolsky and this is Diane." I told them that I had recently read *Love is Letting Go of Fear*, and all they said was, "Thank you." But their genuine warmth filled the tiny converted classroom. I listened to them talk with the reporter and felt that I was in the presence of compassionate genius. Later, when I shared that with my co-worker, she said, "You probably were, and you were also in the presence of unconditional love."

I've never forgotten how it felt to be in the presence of kind and loving strangers that day. I do my best to emulate that ideal of "coming from unconditional love" in all of my daily encounters. Sometimes I fall back into fear, mostly when someone cuts me off on the highway.

I also realized that love is not always welcome in the Boardroom. I'm not talking about romantic love, but about strong affection for another arising out of kinship, personal ties, benevolence or common interests.

Several years ago, I witnessed my friend, David Neenan, tell his employees at a company meeting that he wanted to work with people he loved, and that love was an important element in their working environment. It was a bold step, and one that would be hard to pull off in most corporations where fear rules the hallways and cubicles. But it made sense to me because I had experienced love at two companies – Disney and Intelligent Electronics (IE). The IE Reseller Network Division had evolved from the purchase of a company called Connecting Point in Denver. It was the Connecting Point culture that fostered an environment of love and creativity—to this day the best company I have ever worked for. Sadly, the Connecting Point culture was overcome by IE's more fear-based style, and for a variety of reasons including culture shift, the company started to come apart as turnover rose and creativity dwindled.

Fear is a powerful force. It keeps us in dead-end jobs, or on the road away from our families. It makes us seek more money and power when all we really want is to love and be loved. A short cartoon film titled *Joshua in the Box* beautifully depicts the power of fear to keep us trapped inside boundaries, either real or imagined. The title character, Joshua, is depicted as trapped in a box. He works hard to escape the confines of the box, pushing and shoving until he finally breaks free. Outside of the box, he feels insecure and fearful and is compelled to create another box for himself in order to feel comfortable again.

When we finally escape from our limitations, as Joshua escaped from his "box," we are compelled to create another "box" to keep us safe from the next round of scary changes. We stay in the "box" until we bust out of it and create another, and the cycle continues on and on.

Put love back into the corporation and you imbue it with innovation, creativity, fresh solutions to challenges, energy, enthusiasm and hope. Love gives people permission to be optimistic, to care deeply about their associates and customers, their products and services and their companies. It allows supervisors to listen to workers' concerns without labeling them as weak or ineffective.

I let go of fear when I committed to leave my job and care for my parents. Gary let go of fear when he embraced the idea of moving with me to a new state. Cory and Emilie let go of fear when they chose to move from Cleveland to California to be with our family. Mom and Jack let go of fear when they agreed to stop driving. All of these important decisions were grounded in love.

Someone said to me recently, "hope is everything." I believe that love is everything. After all, love—of something or someone—gives us hope. Love gives us peace. Love gives substance to our caring. Love lights "the heart way" on this journey called life.

Love is patient, Love is kind,
It does not envy, it does not boast,
It is not proud, It is not rude,
It is not self-seeking,
It is not easily angered,
It keeps no record of wrongs.

Love does not delight in evil,
but rejoices with the truth.

Love always protects, always trusts,
always hopes, always perseveres.

Love bears all things, believes all things,
hopes all things, and endures all things.

Love never ends.

LOVE NEVER FAILS.

Corinthians 13 : 4 - 8

APPENDIX A
ELDERCARE RESOURCES

AARP
601 E Street NW
Washington, DC 20049
Phone: 800-424-3410
Web Site: www.aarp.org

AAA Foundation for Traffic Safety
1440 New York Avenue NW, Suite 201
Washington, DC 20005
Phone: 202-638-5944
Web Site: www.aaafts.org

Administration on Aging
330 Independence Avenue SW
Washington, DC 20201
Phone: 202-619-7501
Web Site: www.aoa.gov

Alzheimer's Disease Education and Referral Center (ADEAR)
P.O. Box 8250
Silver Spring, MD 20907
Phone: 800-438-4380
Web Site: www.alzheimers.org

American Association of Homes and Services for the Aging (AAHSA)
2519 Connecticutt Avenue NW,
Washington, DC 20008
Phone: 202-783-2242
Web Site: www2.aahsa.org

Assisted Living Federation of America
11200 Waples Mill Rd, Suite 150
Fairfax, VA 22030
Phone: 703-691-8100
Web Site: www.alfa.org

CareGuide
Phone: 888-389-8839
Web Site: www.careguide.com

Children of Aging Parents
P.O. Box 167
Richboro, PA 18954
Phone: 800-227-7294
Web Site: www.caps4caregivers.org

Eldercare Locator: National Association of Area Agencies on Aging
1730 Rhode Island Avenue NW, Suite 1200
Washington, DC 20036
Phone: 800-677-1116
Web Site: www.eldercare.gov

Health Care Financing Association of America (HIAA)
7500 Security Boulevard
Baltimore, MD 21244
Phone: 410-786-3000
Web Site: www.hcfa.gov

Meals on Wheels Association of America
203 Union Street,
Alexandria, VA 22314
Phone: 800-999-6262
Web Site: www.mowaa.org

Medicare Hotline
Phone: 800-638-6833

National Academy of Elder Law Attorneys
1604 N. Country Club Road
Tucson, AZ 85716
Phone: 520-881-4005
Web Site: www.naela.com

National Adult Day Care Services Association
c/o National Council on the Aging
409 Third Street SW
Washington, DC 20024
800-424-9046
Web Site: www.ncoa.org

National Association of Professional
Geriatric Care Managers
1604 North Country Club Road
Tucson, AZZ 84716
Phone: 520-881-8008
Web Site: www.caremanager.org

National Family Caregivers Association
10400 Connecticut Avenue, Suite 500
Kensington, MD 20895
Phone: 800-896-3650
Web Site: www.thefamilycaregiver.org

National Hospice and Palliative
Care Organization
1700 Diagonal Road, Suite 625
Alexandria, VA 22314
Phone: 800-658-8898
Web Site: www.nhpco.org

Social Security Administration
Office of Public Inquiries
6401 Security Boulevard, Room 4-C-5 Annex
Baltimore, MD 21235
Phone: 800-772-1213
Web Site: www.ssa.gov

Visiting Nurse Associations of America
99 Summer Street, Suite 1700
Boston, MA 02110
Phone: 617-717-3200
Web Site: www.vnaa.org

Work & Family Connection, Inc.
5197 Beachside Drive
Minnetonka, MN 55343
Phone: 800-487-7898
Web Site: www.workfamily.com

APPENDIX B
SUGGESTED READING

Berman, Claire. *Caring for Yourself While Caring for your Aging Parents*. New York: Henry Holt & Co., 1997

Branden, Nathaniel. *How to Raise Your Self-Esteem*. *New York*: Bantam Books, 1987

Breitung, Joan. *The Eldercare Sourcebook*. New York: Contemporary Books, 2002

Cousins, Norman. *Anatomy of an Illness*. New York: W.W. Norton & Co., Inc., 1979

Dyer, Wayne W. *The Power of Intention*. Carlsbad, CA: Hay House, Inc., 2004

Greenberg, Vivian E. *Respecting Your Limits When Caring for Aging Parents*. San Francisco: Jossey-Bass Publishers, 1988

Ilardo, Joseph and Carole Rothman. *Are Your Parents Driving You Crazy?* Acton, MA: VanderWyk & Burnham, 2001

Jampolsky, Gerald, M.D. *Love is Letting Go of Fear*. Berkeley: Celestial Arts, Revised Edition, 1988

Loverde, Joy. *The Complete Eldercare Planner*. New York: Three Rivers Press, 2000

Marcell, Jacqueline. *Elder Rage or Take My Father...Please!* Irvine, CA: Impressive Press, 2001

McGraw, Phillip. *Life Strategies.* New York: Hyperion, 1999

Morse, Sarah, and Donna Quinn Robbins. *Moving Mom and Dad.* Petaluma, CA: Lanier Publishing, 1998.

Orloff, Judith. *Positive Energy.* New York: Harmony Books, 2004

Rhodes, Linda Colvin. *The Complete Idiot's Guide to Caring for Aging Parents.* Indianapolis, IN: Alpha Books, 2001

Seligman, Martin E.P. *Authentic Happiness.* New York: Free Press, 2002

Twichell, Karen. *A Caregiver's Journey: Finding Your Way.* Lincoln, NE: Writers Club Press, 2001

ACKNOWLEDGEMENTS

I made my challenging and rewarding journey with the love and support of family, friends and many invaluable associates. I am profoundly grateful for their participation, collaboration and generous contributions of time and intelligent feedback during the process of writing this book.

First, I want to acknowledge my editors, Kathy Jones and Bobbie Probstein. Your attention to detail and brilliant observations helped to keep me confident and on purpose. Kathy was my original editor at *Orange County Illustrated Magazine* in 1977 and I am fortunate to call her one of my best friends and best mentors to this day.

Anne White, my marvelous designer, co-worker and forever friend, thank you for the gift of your creativity and production expertise, and especially for your unyielding faith in me.

My journey from corporate to care actually began in 1985 with a workshop called *Money & You*, created by my friend, Marshall Thurber. Thank you, Marshall, for your creative spirit that sparked my transformation and nurtures my curiosity to this day. One of Marshall's students, the brilliant and benevolent David Neenan, stepped in to take over the workshop when Marshall stepped out. David created his own version of the seminar, *Business & You*. Thank you, David, for being one of my closest friends and life coaches, and for supporting me in realizing all of my career goals.

Other colleagues and friends during my years

of working in the *Business & You* community contributed to my understanding of the way of the heart. Anne Harwood—my "synergy sister" and partner in so many adventures, Carol and Dan Fetzer, Ruth Ann Hattori and Jim Mikula, Sharon Neenan, Freddi Wilkinson, Margaret McIntyre, Patricia Fox, Allen Mann, Tim Volk, John Graziani, Pam Chambers, Richard Flagg, Steve and Jodi Maero, Bob Bender, Randy Kraft, Eric Lucas, Lee Jensen, Jay Jackman, Myra Strober, Raju Jairam, Bob Medlock, Marilyn Murphy, Ed and Misty Jirikils, Clark Galbreath, Marian Shima, Cheryl Akright and Cata Parkhurst have left a meaningful imprint on my life over the past 20 years, and have shaped the meaning of *What One Man Can Do* in my life.

Michael and LuAnn Curtis, Joe and Mary Lou Whisenand, Della and Ralph Bouwman, Judy Schneider and Victoria Stephens brought me through the grief process as my "safety net" in Colorado. Michael, my cherished "soul brother," has been a remarkable life coach by example. His encouragement in times of painful learning has been nothing less than profound. There are no words to adequately thank these remarkable friends.

I am grateful to my spiritual teachers and psychological counselors—Roger Teel, the late Peggy Bassett, Sandy and Kirk Moore, Doug Olsen, Judy Beadles, Tricia Kelly and Marjorie Bayes. My faith has been buoyed by their wisdom.

I could not have completed this book without the support of my dear friends and associates who were always around with humor, kind words, email jokes, notes of encouragement and invitations—Marianne and Brian Towersey, Terry and Bob Coluccio, Laurie and Barry Booth, Peter Jones, Pete and Kris Glaeser, Cliff and Nancy Hollenbeck, Jeffrey Laymon, Donna Martin, Linda Hazen, Bob Hauptner, Charlene Leep, Claire Manship, Retha Lange, Vicki and Chriss Street, Linda Broderick, Katie Chambers, Barb Boucher, Kathy Hickey, KC Collins, Terry Brodt, Bill and Wendy Johnson, Vin Rosa, Linda Oliver-Eckhardt, Jill Kepler-Fritter, Shelley Gonzales, Lisa Tilley, Bruce and Natalie Eldredge, Jeff and Cheryl Seeley, Nicole and Rick Fierro, Joni Bouveron, Deidre Saterdal, DJ and Dave Greenagel, Lisa Hiatt, Bob Baldwin, Peggy Dursthoff, Sean Glumace, Glenn Talan, Pamela Varga, Marilyn Waidelich, Grant Caplan and Steven Tesney.

I want to acknowledge the people who inspired me in my career and helped me to sharpen my focus and learn to navigate the tumultuous world of corporate marketing and communications. Thank you, Ron Cruger, Sharon Weiner, Michael Bullis, Bob McTyre, Mark Feary, Jack Lindquist, the late Hideo Amemiya, Mark Briggs, Tim Jeffries, Thom Nulty and Gina Keating. You have helped to shape who I am today.

There are many family members and lifelong family friends who have stood by me in good and bad times, and without whom my family would not be as strong as it is today. Thank you, Ellie and David Fraser, Margie MacNair, Dick and Carla MacNair, Janet and Roy Dohner, Jill and Mike Short, Anne Nelson, Gaye Nelson,

Shannon Cottrell, Nancy Sumner, Geraldine Toltschin, Arline and Chuck Johnson, Judy and Gary Valentine, Bettie Sill, Marilyn and Davy Crockett, Porge and Carl Nilsen, Barbara Campbell Ramsey, Keith and Lillian Lumpkin, Jean, Brad, Karen, Bill and Emmy Baker, Pat, Denise, Joseph and Piper Bartels, MM and Margo Haeckle, Howard, Donna and Jeffrey MacNair, Maureen Hales, Sue Kasler, Price MacNair, Evelyn, Robert and Kathleen Walker and Janine and Steve Anderson.

My day-to-day supporters and the people who have helped my parents and me during our learning experience of eldercare deserve my utmost gratitude—Dr. James Berman, Dr. Sasha Thomas, Dr. Michael Yu, Dr. Kathleen Hutton, Rosie Trujillo, Kathy Gambaro, Callie Rutter, Ceil Fitzpatrick, Celina Flores, Roxanne Berenbeim, Darlene Mann, Grace Abaya, Jean Galloway, Randy Byrnes, Denise Smith, Rick Hoting, Roy Leonard, Amy Barrozo, Chris Kelly, Dana Ostrander, Sunny Sandhu, Paul Shimoff, Wendy Herring, Lisa Adam, Rita Kurtz, Maria Vanlandingham, Elisol McKim, Evelyn Shull, Marcia Wise, Philip Barklow, Ruth Williamson and the wonderful staffs of the Inn at the Park Senior Community in Irvine, CA and Mesa Verde Convalescent Hospital in Costa Mesa, CA.

I want to thank the members of my "learning community," The Inside Edge, for blessing my life with something to look forward to every Wednesday morning, namely discovery, fellowship and unconditional love. Special thanks to Larry Maurer, Carol Edmonston, Jim Collister, Joanne Tatham, June Crockett, Gil

Mahlmeister, Cathy Bateman, Jane Drew, Joan Linder, Jeanne Michele, Lois Nightengale, Kathy Blank, Charlotte Backman, Gail Brooks, Ardis Freeman, Paul Gadebusch, Kathy Gardarian, Diana Wentworth, Lisa Cherney, Floren Harper, John Russell, Marion Barrons, Kate Griffith, Bill Cleminshaw, Ruth Cooper, Audre Braggins, Shawn Bos, Mary Ree, Ruthanne Ali, Sharon Forrest, Brook Cross, Toby Larson, Jane Kennedy, Jean-Pierre Swinnen, Mary Joosten, Steve Blackburn, Denise Fager, Kevin Roberts, Arline Hodges, Marilyn Graves, Susen Kay, Rich Freschi, Chet Brisco, Suzy Giraud, Judy Kelsey, Keith Garrison, Loy Geddes, Jim Morris, Karen Phelps, Suzy Casey, Maria Rowe, Elaine Regan, Jane Wolf, Denise Quinn, Lea Timmons, Pat Verbeck, Michael Coleman, Odile Nicolette, Adrian Windsor and "Gorby." If I missed any of you, it's because we don't know each other yet!

Many of my life's most exciting and exquisite journeys have been shared with someone I am most grateful to call my dearest friend—my cousin, Dru Cottrell. Thank you, Dru, for being there at every difficult and vulnerable moment and every celebration in my life. I promise to stay at wonder with you so that we never get bored or complacent.

Finally, I want to acknowledge my family: my extraordinary sister, Meg Garner Johnson, her husband, Ted Johnson, and their precious daughter, Hannah. We do great holiday meals! My brother, John Sumner, has been my treasured friend since childhood, and continues to occupy a special place in my heart as we grow older and make more and more difficult choices.

Thank you to my niece and "rent-a-kid," Lindsey Sumner, who lights up my life with love, a sense of adventure, and the important knowledge of all things hip. And to my amazing stepson, Cory Ingram, and his beautiful wife, Emilie, who gave me the incredible gift of knowing, at last, what it means to be a mom and a grandma. Thank you to my grandson, Keegan Ingram, for endless hours of entertainment and joy.

My parents, the remarkable and resilient Marianne and Jack Garner and the late John J. Sumner, gave me the gifts of life and love and helped to shape my own unique perspective. I am profoundly grateful to Mom and Jack for teaching me about patience and the challenges of aging gracefully, and for allowing me to be their caregiver for a couple of wild and crazy years.

I send my deep gratitude to the late Bruce Stewart, my beloved first husband, for giving me an independent spirit, self-confidence, worldly wisdom and undying curiosity about life and its lessons. I am fortunate to have been married to two incredible men, and Bruce will always be in my heart.

Last but most important of all, I am grateful to Gary Ingram, my husband, partner, best friend and love of my life. Thank you for your vulnerability, integrity, humor, strength, respect, boundless love, and for making me believe that anything is possible.

THE HEART WAY .... A JOURNEY FROM CORPORATE TO CARE

BOOK ORDER FORM

Web Site Orders: www.shannoningram.com

Mail Orders: (Please Print)

Name _____

Address _____ _

City _____

State _____ Zip _____

Phone _____

email _____

Ordering/Billing Information

Number of Books _____ @ $14.95

Shipping Cost
(1-2 Books - $4 *per* book; 3-10 books - $3 *per* book)

Total Cost (Books + Shipping) _____

Send Check or Money Order to:
Orren Stewart Press
427 E. 17th St., Suite F-230
Costa Mesa, CA 92627

Please send more FREE information on:
☐ Speaking/Seminars
☐ Other Books/Articles by Shannon Ingram

www.shannoningram.com